IMAGES FOR GOLF

visualizing your way to a better game

Dr. Geoffrey Lucas

The Publisher: **Arizona Academic Sport Resources**
116 Edgewood Drive, N.W.,
Calgary, Alberta, Canada T3A 2T5

Typeset in Garth Graphic by
Résistance Typographers, Edmonton.
Printed by Commercial Colour Press.
Cover Illustration: Christopher Heatherington
Inside Illustrations: Kim Johansen

Canadian Cataloguing in Publication Data
Lucas, Geoffrey, 1940 —
Images for Golf

Bibliography: p.
1. Golf.   2. Visualization.   I. Title.
GV965.L83 1987   796.352'3   C87-091214-3
ISBN 0-9692902-0-9

Table of Contents

Chapter 1
The Brain, Imagery and Sports

Chapter 2
Imagery and Mental Skills as Used by Professional Golfers

Chapter 3
Introduction to Imagexercise© Golf

Chapter 4
Improving Your Image Making Ability

Appendix

Bibliography and Resources

Preface

The success of *Images For Golf: Visualizing your way to a better game*, will be measured by the extent to which the golfer gains the skills and knowledge required for mind control golf.

Almost surely golfers will reduce their average golf game score but the more important factor will be the extent to which they gain satisfaction at golf. If future instruction for the training and education of mental golf is improved this may also serve as a signal that the book's ideas are working.

I have enjoyed the opportunity to lay before the reader the critical knowledge and applications that are required to augment the continuous improvement of golf skills. Moreover, the opportunity to work with golf classes and unique individuals at all levels of golf skill, with golf camp groups of all ages on imagery amd golf enhancement, and with top ranked amateurs has been inspirational. This is an exciting new sport field! Golfers recognize that improved golf is often mind control golf.

Future work with top flight Tour players will uncover other unique imagery visualization applications. The long list of Tour golfers with special mind control skills will grow. To the list of Horton Smith, Jack Nicklaus, Johnny Miller, Sylvia Bertoluccini, Denis Watson, Ben Hogan, Johnny Revolta, Jack Fleck, Al Geiberger, Bobby Jones, Tom Watson, Nancy Lopez, Hal Sutton, Kathy Hite, Dick Zokal, Patty Sheehan, Greg Norman, Jay Haas, Joan

Joyce, George Knudson, Jack Renner, Penny Pulz, Peter Jacobsen, Lee Trevino, Ray Floyd and Cary Middlecoff will come other great mind control golfers.

Scientists of sport, sport psychologists, optometrists, P.G.A. professionals, and certified imagery professionals have all supported the development of this type of book. Further research, as recently as this past summer has shown that the imagery exercises of the last chapter of this book are effective in improving the putting abilities of men, women, and junior golfers.

Images For Golf: Visualizing your way to a better game follows three natural subdivisions. The first subdivision is known loosely as the present status, science and current use by Tour professionals of golf imagery. The second natural subdivision includes the operations of imagery in golf as the golfer develops *Tactics, Tenacity* and *Techniques* for golf. The third subdivision contains the plans and exercises for imagery skill practice and basic improvement.

The increased interest in the acquisition of imagery skill by golfers everywhere has been coaxed along and accompanied by volumes of writing and literature, all in such an unrelated form that a reader is somewhat at a loss in gaining in depth detail for regularizing imagery golf. The placing of all imagery golf ideas in one book is an attempt to remedy this fragmentation of information.

Imagination, it is said* is by far the most neglected and underdeveloped area of the mind. Some people have photographic memories but the majority of people need assistance in developing such skill. It is also said that a psychotherapist expects you to use imagery to explore better ways of developing a stable mind. Rarely do we consider the creative potential of imagery.

The images of worry and concern try to intrude on our images and even our specific sport images and that is why our book stresses applying needed, rehearsed imagery through exercising golf images. Twenty-five percent of the population are capable of reasonably good visual images but just 10 percent can claim intense, real-as-life, vivid, visual images.

This book is an attempt to alter this bleak statistic among golfers. Golfers can change this statistic.

Tour professionals are currently working with sport psychologists and are among those athletes who frequently take a week off to attend workshops or other intensive mental golf re-education or development efforts. Details of these recent efforts and suggestions for any golfer's improvement will be the main stress of *Images For Golf*. Mental golf may be the wave of the future, but it is the present stress of up-to-the-minute golfers.

Generally speaking, image ability in golf combines with other success factors such as recently acquired correction of swing flaws or game procedures, game management, aiming, aligning and shot procedures.

No matter at what level of golf or sport fitness you are at presently, you too can benefit from procedures and programs for improving your Pure Imagery Skill and Golf Score enhancement.

A Word About the Golfers' Commitment

The program of image improvement and application in this book is called Imagexercise© or the practice of developing and using imagery to improve your golf swing, your ability in the tactics of golf and the mental tenacity you bring to the golf course for your golf game participation. The program involves a modest investment of time and effort. A few hours per week during the pre-season, about the same hours during the golf season and a few minutes during the critical post game time will be sufficient. The time commitment is ongoing and active rather than a one-time only reading or practice.

My deepest appreciation is expressed to my fellow Faculty members and Administrators at The University of Calgary, Alberta, Canada for sharing increased workloads during terms of leave thus allowing book projects to reach fruition. Appreciation is also directed towards golfing associates and teaching experts in the Scottsdale, Arizona area, to my typists, to the two graphic artists, to Resistance Graphics, to proofreaders and idea users and to the small Sports System Computer usage group at my own University. Lastly, my thanks to the Professional Golfers of the United States and Canada. My especial thanks to CPGA professionals of Alberta and British Columbia.

W.G.L.

---

* Barbara Brown. *Supermind: The Ultimate Energy.* New York: Harper and Row, 1980.

Introduction

True imagers have developed a rather amazing degree of detail in their images. Their images or mind's eye pictures (that is, brain generated pictures which flash through the mind) can have vividness, color, detail and timing. An image can be held momentarily in the brain and images occur frequently to a user.

An image can, and often does, involve many basic senses such as feel, sight, smell, touch and taste. And images can be improved!

While almost every human being has some ability to create and use images, there are great fluctuations in ability from person to person. Scientists, philosophers, musicians, artists and doodlers, educators and story tellers, entertainers, athletes, bright-minded people and healthy, physically fit people all tend to be imagers.

So do injured and imprisoned people who have provided us with some outstanding examples of image ability and application. Some occupations and some life skills, particularly, require image creation ability.

Imagery is a slightly more complex field of learning than you might at first suppose. Good imagery may provide you with some amazing learning and lifestyle dividends.

Introduction and a
Self-Analysis of your Imagery

How often have you used an image to direct your action in your present lifestyle? Are you driving a car or are you in a sport situation when images occur to you? Do you see images or mind's eye pictures when you are thinking through a problem.

Perhaps mind's eye pictures happen to you in connection with hunches or intuitive thinking. But more than likely your images have to do with reactions or emergency situations when a quick mind's eye picture precedes some rapid and often brilliant reaction by yourself!

Have you had the experience of seeing your whole life history flash before your eyes when you found yourself in a jam or death-arousing scare or situation? If you have had to dive underwater to rescue someone or were pulled underwater by a dangerous current, you probably had a detailed series of mind's eye pictures or movie style images bombard your brain.

Perhaps you have had less traumatic experiences such as a leisurely relaxed afternoon lying in some favorite spot where you preview and review your future plans in life or in sport life. Have you found your imagery to be *accurate*? Are your images in *technicolor*? Are your images *frequent*? Are your images *rare*?

If you have had any of the above images, you most certainly may be able to generate and apply images in sport that will dramatically improve your performance!

"The training you do in your imagination is the same as the real physical training as far as your brain is concerned."

Bennett and Pravitz. *The Miracle of Sports Psychology* (1).

Brain-Game Golf
Up To 1978

Brain function research and the science of mental process and mental function has provided us with a wealth of new information since the 1960s and 1970s. This information has been used by educators, psychologists and by golf-educators to provide us with an exceptional amount of learning theory and golf learning.

Marilyn Ferguson, a futurist, speaker and author of the *Aquarian Conspiracy*, has put the situation this way, "the brain's right and left hemispheres interact all the time, but each has certain functions of its own" (2).

Marilyn Ferguson

In sport, the left hemisphere is an analyzer among its other jobs, and the right hemisphere is an image and skill "feel" selector among its other jobs. Injuries confined to one side of the brain have been studied to enhance brain hemisphere knowledge. Sophisticated brain study techniques were also developed. In addition, twenty-five split-brain surgery cases among severe epilepsy patients further contributed to a knowledge of brain function. The connection between the two hemispheres (the bridge or corpus collusome) in the cases noted was severed in the hope of confining brain seizures to one side of the brain and body.

This type of patient was studied so that function and sidedness, if such existed, was clearly differentiated.

These Functions Are Summarized As Follows:

Left Side Brain Particularly in Sport	Right Side Brain Particularly in Sport
▪ names, compartmentalized	▪ "thinks" in images
▪ takes "snapshots" and "fits" information	▪ sees whole
	▪ more musical and emotional tone
▪ deals with the past	▪ watches "movies"
▪ awareness	▪ completes the
▪ analyzes	▪ gestalts

Left Brain
Right Brain

Integrated Brain System

For "brain game" putting, short shots and regular shots. Integrated via "whole brain knowing." The right brain or the performance selector brain uses its image selector to formulate images from the image monitor. *Images regulate performance.*

The following chart summarizes some of what we know about brain function, particularly for sport participation, image generation and *Imagexercise©*. Additional new theories of brain function were developed after 1978. Until then it had been in vogue to discuss the brain's hemispheres or sides (as if they were "separate" entities). The "whole" brain idea suffered. So that, relative to brain side function, be aware that the sides of the brain are joined and except in the case of surgery, always have been! The "joining" creates something new. Whole brain knowing is far more than the sum of its parts and "different from either."

Whole Brain knowing and our golf score

*As golfers, we want to know what the "Hemispheres" or sides can do for our golf game but we do play with the "**Whole Brain**"!*

When properly applied, knowledge of brain function cuts our golf score.

Brain Function
Particularly golf function

Left Brain	**Right Brain**
"Analyzer"	Performance Selector or Intuition and Integration

"Corpus"
Connecting Bridge

Functions	**Functions**
▪ names, organizes,	▪ thinks in images
▪ compartmentalizes	▪ sees wholes
▪ takes "snapshots" and "fits" information	▪ more musical and emotional tones
▪ deals with the past	▪ watches "movies"
▪ awareness	▪ completes the gestalt

Subconscious process performs overlearned skill, i.e., golf swing

Subconscious process Golf swing

Whole Brain Function

"Brain Game Golf"

Exercise three main images for golf

Certainly imagery itself, making decisions and executing them in golf are whole brain. Despite this, we use our brain sidedness for analysis which is a left brain function. Seeing the "whole" and selecting our performance and how it should feel involves the right brain in particular. The subconscious, a different level of brain function, actually performs the swing.

Richard Coop and Gary Wiren (3) have brought together the information about sides of the brain and golf and labelled their ideas (and book) the *New Golf Mind*. They have said that golfers often blame swing mechanics for a bad shot when, in fact, the golfer's mind may be keeping the body from performing effectively. This would happen if the golfer was still analyzing during the actual swing procedure. This is easily seen when we change our mind or are undecided halfway into a golf swing. Coining expressions such as *"Analyzer Golf"* and *"Integrator Golf,"* they have shown golfers when to use them. This information and application should be considered mandatory if you wish to save strokes. Mandatory because their ideas can so easily be seen to affect the golfer.

Tactics Imagexercise© and *Technique Imagexercise©* are also ways of dealing with golf information. They culminate in clearly defined pictures in our brains. Pictures or images which eliminate confusion in the brain of the golfer. There can be no confusion since images must be formed before performance can commence. Only then do you start performing. *Tactics* and *Imagexercise©*always come first in shot procedure.

Tactics, once decided upon, completes the left brain's job. Analysis is over! The right brain selects the shot decided upon, and calls to your swing techniques or swing mechanics to complete the shot. The right brain works on feel and "muscle memory" to get ready for the swing. It duplicates the image picture with your body's lever and muscular system. *So Technique Imagexercise© takes over.* It uses your selected image as a model. Your muscle memory and you complete the shot. The performance of the shot itself is controlled by the brain's subconscious function or the lower brain cortex.

The idea of using imagery had always been around in golf. For example, Ben Hogan learned golf swing movements and maintained his swing via pictures or mirror images repeated hundreds of times. He said that by doing this he could recall exact swing positions out on the golf course. Hogan called this the "coming attraction" way of learning golf. Besides mirrors, he used movie newsreel "clips" of golfers and their swings long before videotapes came along. It is said that when Hogan booked a motel room, he made sure mirrors were present in the room.

Hogan's "Coming Attraction" or imagery

Sports imagery gained some real reemphasis and more widespread use when news stand journals such as *Psychology Today* reported its use among psychologists and athletes. Olympic athletes, especially from Europe and the Communist bloc, appeared to have a mental edge. National sport governing bodies in the U.S.A., the U.K., Australia, Japan, Sweden and Canada began to incorporate basic psychological information into programs designed to educate coaches of youth sports. Thus some basic ideas of mental training emerged. Since the early 1970s, physical educators have been well versed in the content of basic sports psychology. It soon became apparent than any "edge" rested solely with the individual golfer or athlete.

Types of Images for Golf

There will be hundreds of examples of images presented to you in this book. Primarily, we expect to propose images of four types that have been suggested or used by professional golfers, golf instructors and sports psychologists. The exact nature of the images may vary, yet they have functioned for someone out there. The images you select may vary considerably. One image may not work, for example, for another person in your golf foursome. It is not the image but rather the quality of it and the "exercise" or purpose that will initiate improvement. Imagery will work!

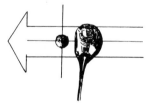

Types of Images for Golf

External Imagery
Any mind's eye image that could be provided by a movie camera but instead is provided by your mind-camera (external).

Internal Imagery
Any mind's eye image of your inner feeling such as a good stretch, the good feel of a complete shoulder turn or your hands maintaining a firm and tender connection with the club.

Cognitive Imagery
Any mind's eye image of you as an analytical golfer. For example, you see yourself as a golfer who corrects a swing fault or game procedure after the game (sometimes during) so that you do not repeat mistakes.

Affective Imagery
Any mind's eye image about your attitude to and awareness of yourself and others. For example, you see an image of a clear plan that calls for you to play the course and not your opponent. You also see yourself considering each shot you play as requiring your best effort.

Most experienced golfers who use imagery will agree upon the following characteristics for imagery. Not all the characteristics occur together. Note that the characteristics suggest a variety of purposes. This is not visual thinking, a skill that most of us possess. It is beyond visual thinking. It is as if real mental pictures existed.

Naturally, as in any skill, the ability to create powerful mental pictures or images needs to be taught and practiced regularly. It will be the business of our book to teach you about imagery and enable you to present powerful images for your golf game.

Correct regular practice and effective imagery

The Characteristics of Imagery
Basic Expectations for Your Imagery

Vividness

Does your mind's eye image have clarity and accuracy? Does it include the details you require? Is your image missing some parts?

Self or other

Is your image of your own swing or a model? Is the model suitable? Does the model seem realistic to you?

Color

Is the image in shades of grey, reds, blacks and whites or do you image in technicolor?

Tense

Does your image complete itself? In tracking the path of a ball, do you see the start, the middle and the end of a ball's flight? Do you see the landing and the direction of the bounce? Do you see the ball fall into the hole?

Timing

Can you "call up" the image that you need for the situation at the correct instant in time?

Speed

Does a movement in your image take place at full speed? Can you use "frame by frame" images?

Animation

Some images require qualities suggested by music or by an animal. The golf wind-up is like getting ready to "spring like a tiger." A whistle or hum builds timing.

Tempo

Does your image allow you to feel or duplicate accelerating motion? Does it use onomatopoeia like an "oomm-pah"! or a six-count swing with a slow 1-2-3 and a faster 4-5-6? Can you hum your image?

Smoothness

Imagery for a long putt stroking action may benefit you much more if it is based on a smoothness cue, "oily smooth" or "custard stirring smooth"!

Movement
Is your image moving? Do you see, hear and feel yourself moving?

Positive-Negative
Does your image suggest a golf "disaster"? Re-image to a positive image in case it does!

Body Reaction
Imagery is accompanied by actually firing off a small muscle force in your body. Do you feel tingling or tightening? Do you feel relaxed?

Image-Endurance
Can you image on Holes 16, 17 and 18? Do you give up on your imagery too soon?

Purposes of Imagery for Golf
Three Main Applications of *Imagexercise*©

In introducing the reader to *Imagexercise*© you will find that imagery is categorized in three ways:

Technique Imagery

Start developing the three main types of imagery

Provides models of the golf swing for your body type and body movements. For example, four clear accurate mind's eye pictures for stance, top of the backswing prior to ball striking and follow through. The best method is to paste up these four on a small card and to start collecting a bank or file of swing images.

Tactics Imagery
Provides models of the golf course you are playing, just like seeing a mini movie of each hole. Minimum suggested is an image of landing area, hazards, locations and slopes around the greens.

Tenacity Imagery
Provides standards of desire in your golf game. For example, being tough enough with yourself that you see yourself doing the three key things to make good putts on each hole (stroke rehearsal for form and speed; read the green; complete the plan in striking the ball).

Also commonly used to carry out the tougher shots that are less frequent in a game. Build concentration and consistency.

Initial Use of *Technique Imagexercise*©

Many experienced golfers suggest that the three main purposes of imagery in golf are as noted earlier. When learning golf for the first time, you likely will find most use for *Technique Imagexercise*©. In introductory golf classes, of twenty-one hours, we stress this technique. Because our students like to play golf as soon as possible, we follow a guideline that might work well for you. After the first ten to twelve hours of basic swing practice, rules, golf procedures and etiquette, we move into *Tactics* imagery without further delay. We suggest doing this in one of two ways.

Starting To Use *Tactics Imagexercise*©

Pick out a simple nine hole golf course, one that has wide fairways that are basically flat, and has lots of "character" around the greens. That is, some slopes, some sand traps, some banked aprons and, if possible, large or at least medium-sized greens. The total length of the nine hole course should be short.

Start With *Tactics Imagexercise*©

First, scout the course twice by playing orientation games. These games are for the purpose of rehearsing your imagery. If possible, play with someone who knows the course and knows the type of shots you presently hit. Note the landing areas from the tee, close your eyes and mentally review these areas. Use a score card map and xxx out the best landing areas. Golf students in classes play the first games with three clubs, a small coiled paper book that is pocket size, a pencil and a couple of golf balls. Next, as you walk up to the greens, note the slopes and the contours. Take note of the preferred landing areas or bounce and run-up areas. While waiting for your turn to hit,

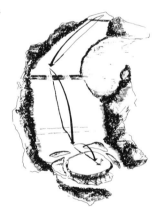

Gaining the advantage on the golf course

St. Andrews: an example of Tactics Imagery

Imagexercise© these spots in your mind. Play your shot. After three holes, pause with your group, let the golfers behind play through if the course ahead of you is empty, and make a few very brief notes or place some symbols in your book. After the game, save your notes and mentally run through your *Tactic Imagexercise*© before playing again.

The second method is equally simple. Someone draws up a simple map of the nine holes and runs you through a series of *Imagexercise*© consisting of two images per hole (one for each teebox and green situation). This can be done with your group as you pause from your lesson or practice. When you play you will re-work your notes and re-image as much as possible.

Experienced Golfer Using *Tactics Imagexercise*©

There are equally systematic ways of using *Tactics Imagexercise*© for more experienced golfers playing a new golf course. A golfer suggested the following. After playing the "Eden" course at St. Andrews, Scotland, for which he knew Tactics Imagery, he pre-scouted the "New Course" later in the afternoon, when few golfers were teeing off. Never having played the "New Course" but needing to know it for an upcoming local tournament, he discovered the secret of how the architect designed each hole. Every fairway on the "New Course" consists of ground contours of continuous dips, hillocks and uneven terrain. But, wonder of wonders, at exactly 180-185 yards out for men, and 150-155 yards for ladies, there is a large-sized flat landing area. Any shot landing on this flat area bounces true and runs true to a stop on an excellent flat area from which you can play your next shot (alas, however, any shot not landing as the course architect intended bounces untrue and heads for the nearest gorse growth, usually ending up suspended three inches or so off the ground, often unplayable!).

As you approach the greens on the "New Course" at St. Andrews, you will be able to take note of an equally intelligent approach strategy for playing up to the greens. Make this the basis for your *Imagexercise*© tactics. Each fairway on the "New Course" follows an identical pattern of landing areas. The golf course is admirably fair to the golfer and makes your tactical approach and your imagery extremely effective. Of course, it eventually boils down to a challenging game of *Tactic Imagexercise*©, *Technique Imagexercise*©, and striking your shot. All in all, not that easy but, at least, a demanding golfing challenge.

Most experienced golfers and sports psychologists agree on the following advice for learning Tactics and Imagery. They have been known to say (and we agree), learn one golf course so well that your imagery and your golf game can combine to build great confidence in golf. It is advisable, for example, to learn in a golf environment where you can come to express fully your self-knowledge and your potential for golf. A week to ten days playing the four courses at St. Andrews, Scotland can be a learning experience that will amaze you. Play the "Eden" and the beachfront "Jubilee" every day and occasionally switch to the "New Course" and the "Old Course." This is the way to learn.

Looking back to page eight for the purposes of imagery in golf, you can look forward to utilizing the final main purpose of *Imagexercise*© in golf, the *Tenacity Imagexercise*©.

Being tough with the standards you demand of yourself on the golf course, or as you practice will be discussed thoroughly in Chapter 3.

Sport psychologists suggest the following general purposes for imagery and *Imagexercise*©.

The General Purposes

1. To improve your golf technique, tactics and tenacity.

2. To build your confidence

A bonus of golf learnings through imagery

3. To build your *Self-Efficacy* or the strength of your conviction that you can improve (see Bandura in a later chapter).

4. To augment the learning of new skills.

5. To reduce your reliance on the written word. (You can become visual instead of verbal!)

6. To change a bad habit.
7. To improve the consistency of your performance.
8. To play as close to your full potential as possible.
9. To prepare *Interventions*. That is, to develop and pre-practice skills and strategies for all or many of the situations you will be confronted with on the golf course. For example, you will never learn to hit a shot from deep grass on the golf course. Accurately learn the image and the shot skills beforehand.

Interventions is a key

General Purposes of *Imagexercise*©

The main purpose of this book is to start or initiate your personal imagery program. The most common way is *Technique Imagexercise*©.

As you get more and more into your use of *Imagexercise*© you will find that your confidence and conviction will grow. *Imagexercise*© is also used to develop new skills when being able to image shot shape and shot mechanics is basic. You will capitalize on this more and more as you become visually oriented (for example, study of the next issue of your favorite golf magazine should be highly visual and the explanations will not even be used except for further development of your imagery and skills). Bad habits can be changed or replaced and overall consistency will change. Of course, you will play golf at a level chosen as your true potential. Finally, expect to develop your interventions and avoid previous golf disasters!

Can Imagery Work for Introductory or Occasional Golfers?

Occasional golfers as imagery users

A research report read at the Los Angeles Pre-Olympic Scientific Congress claimed that imagery used prior to hitting golf shots by *occasional* golfers improved accuracy of 5 iron shots hit to a target green by an effective distance reduction of eight feet. However, pure *introductory* golfers did not exhibit very much improvement. *Occasional* golfers usually golfed at least once a week and had nearly completed a second university golf class of twenty-one hours duration. The golfers made sure they could "see" an image of one of three random and fundamental golf positions. The images were viewed just prior to starting the swing. The images were shown to the golfers in the form of colored pictures of well-known golfers in distinctive swing positions.

Introductory golfers could not hit consistent golf shots and reported that they could not use imagery because of too much "reminder-type" thinking. Beginners had to remember to do such and such (remember to watch the ball, remember to swing slowly, and so on). Imagery creates a brain overload for *introductory* golfers.

The same research report investigated *Tactics* imagery as used by *occasional* golfers and reported that such imagery (called game management imagery) can contribute to golf score reduction. The reduction of score was reported as eight strokes in an eighteen hole game. The golfers kept journals which showed that the imagery actually was functioning. Remember, however, that the golfers were improving in accuracy of shots at the same time, so that some of the improvement was due to that fact. The reasons why this can occur will be outlined in the further chapters. The composition of *Tactic Imagexercise*© or the game management used in the reported research is as found in the following chart.

Using Tactics images reduces score

Composition of Game Management Imagery used in Level II Golf Instruction

Game Management I
Imagery exercises to review key landing areas, contours and situations of a golf course.

Game Management II
Imagery exercises to review contours of all apron areas near greens.

Game Management III
Imagery exercises to review slopes and overall shapes of greens.

Manage your game in four ways

Game Management IV
Journal entries done post-game to record actual game shots and check on imagery and off-imagery performance.

Mental Practice Session

Many investigators have reported that mental practice can be effective for a variety of motor skills.

What is mental practice in sport?

Mental practice occurs through instruction to mentally rehearse a skill without associated physical (or overt) practice. For example, a basketball player (of any skill level) might imagine a foul shooting motion complete with a feel for the position, the motion, the "lift" and the tempo and arm "wrist finger action," as the imaginary ball is delivered in a shot.

Considerable physical-mental learning occurs as a result. Schmidt (5), a motor learning specialist, has called the mental practice a curious phenomenon but has assured us that the phenomenon has been studied throughout this century. Mental practice produces a large positive transfer to the actual skill. For years this practice has been utilized by good instructors and coaches in sport and physical education. Typical experiments show that an imagery-visualization procedure practiced over days two to nine in a ten-day experiment provides as much improvement as a physical practice program.

The skills used are usually not as complex as a golf swing, but tend to be more of the "arm motion," pursuit rotor task (following a target with the hand) or the like. The experiments show that what is learned is the "sequence" of the task and the particular throwing action or hitting action is not as evidently improved by the mental practice. Since the sequence elements are required in the early stages of acquiring a skill, mental practice is usually more effective in early practice or by beginners.

The research on mental practice, then, is not in total agreement with research as reported by Lucas (6) and others, since the benefits have been found to occur to beyond beginning performances. Suinn

(1980) also reports skill improvement in "apparent contradiction" to basic mental practice findings. We are talking only of the issue of the levels of the learners, not of the benefit.

We are told that there are many unanswered and important theoretical questions. There are critical experiments still to be done. Readers, however, may rest assured that imagery, whether as a pure form of learning or, as is more likely, in combination form with physical practice, is quite likely to improve their performance.

You might think of it in this way. The combination may be imagery plus attention to self or imagery plus self-confidence or imagery plus accurate information for proper brain function.

Imagery Is A Part of Golf Improvement

Each performer may need a slightly different combination of imagery and physical practice in order for imagery to be maximally effective. Often imagery is best done along with relaxation techniques. In fact, you cannot force imagery. Imagery is indeed a part of athletic training and is as effective as a real physical training combination as far as your brain is concerned. Dorothy Harris (7), a noted sports psychologist, says that imagery practice is more effective with highly skilled athletes but it can be used at any skill level.

Imagery requires relaxation

The basic mental practice research just mentioned has separated physical practice from mental practice for experimental purposes only. In real life, in real practice and in real golf, we will not be concerned with "separating" the two aspects.

That is, one will follow the other, as already explained, in an ever repeating cycle of effective golf performance. Once imagery drops off performance will tend to drop off as well. During mental practice we are inadvertently doing physical practice within our muscle fibers. The notion that we "think with our muscles" will be explained next.

Scientific Reasons for Imagery Effectiveness

"There remains considerable conjecture as to the reason or reasons for physical improvement after utilization of mental practice or covert rehearsal techniques, regardless of the immediacy of follow-up physical performance. Three types of explanations exist (5). Mental practice may provide learning of cognitive elements of the task, especially rapid learning of sequences and timing. Second, there may be actual small muscle forces firing off during mental practice and internal feedback at a very high level in the Central nervous System. Third, mental practice may set arousal level and generally get a performer ready for a good attempt or performance. Although definitive explanations are still forthcoming, the prospects of using imagery for sport and physical education in teaching - learning situations are immense. Brain research will likely provide further answers in the future."

Schmidt's scientific explanation

The statement that there *may* be actual small muscle forces firing off during imagery and internal feedback at a very high level in the central nervous system should be a stronger statement. Edmund Jacobsen (8), a doctor who studied imagery and relaxation in the 1930s, confirmed that actual small muscle forces were aroused during these states. If you have started a stimulation by imagining or visualizing in the CNS you have set off a pattern via an impulse, and the pattern is associated with that action. It is said that the more you practice imagining a certain skill and calling up the pattern, the more effective and efficient the imagery and action becomes.

Barbara Brown (9), in her book, Supermind, called imagination the ultimate energy. She reinforces what has been said in this book by saying that imagery is a "neglected and underdeveloped" ability of humans. Almost nothing is known about how to develop an imagery strategy to assist improvement in performance. Brown gave two important clues. A detailed and specific image gives a specific effect. You can excite and generate specific impulses. This means that you can recall former performances of your own and improve upon them. *Second,* imagining can make your body work. The body responds exactly to the image. One day, for example, while watching the Touring professionals hit golf balls at the Phoenix Open, I was imagining hitting balls as well as a hero of mine, Dick Stockton. My muscles reponded. I started swinging. Stockton walked over and asked me what I was doing! He stayed for five minutes and gave me one of the best golf lessons I have ever had. This notion, literally thinking with our muscles and nervous system, has enormous implications in sport and in other ways.

Dick Stockton

Knowing More About What You Image

Earlier we noted that the basic imagery for golf has to do with *Technique*. This is, no doubt, due to the fact that good swing action is based on some fundamentals that are universally necessary. These fundamentals are very well known but difficult to acquire. Let us say that one of them is posture, another is accelerating motion and tempo in general, and a third is swinging through or simply swinging, not hitting. Clearly, to establish your ability to create effective images you will need image-making ability itself and then a ''creative monitor'' of many accurate swing pictures upon which to draw. The more swing pictures you can recall to imagery and the more detailed they are, the more you can benefit from such imagery.

Chapter 4 will improve your image making via exercises especially if your mind's eye is presently devoid of golf images.

Why do you think great *tour* professionals have great balance and great acceleration control? Try to figure it out! Experiment! Test out your theories and guesses. What are the reasons for great golf balance? Are footwork and knee action reduced by body height during striking or rotation?

You can build up images for balance. Balance soon improves and your consistent striking of golf

Build up your images

Golf is not only repeating skills

shots may surprise you! Start by using your scissors and your old golf magazines. Paste up some good balanced swing examples on cards. "Image them" and work on them. Make your body do the interpretive work. Use mirrors constantly. Your body will connect with your central nervous system. You will learn an enormous amount about good balance during a golf motion. Eventually you will see that just one favorite image will provide you with all you need to know about balance. The one image will *cue* you in and will represent all the correct muscle forces firing off via your imagery system. The more often and the more accurate the image, the better your balance will become! *But* you must build your confidence that this is so!

Dorothy V. Harris of Penn State University has summarized the point we are talking about. The more you know about what you are imagining, the more effectively you will be able to practice those skills. Golfers are relatively lucky because their sport consists of basic and repeated variations of the same swinging motion. Sports experts label golfers "closed loop skill participants." In tennis, by contrast, you react to an opponent who gives you a changing situation each time. Team sports involve all kinds of additional dimensions but imagery practice can be useful there as well.

Some readers and golf experts may disagree! Let me say that I do not consider golf a game of repeating motor skills (my swing never repeats itself in exactly the same way!!!) as much as sports experts suggest it is. One illustration will explain my idea. Because golf challenges me in so many ways, and because I do not want to "invent" new shots on the golf course, my practice is totally variable. For example, when using my wedge for practice around our putting green, I hit low ones, high ones, lazy ones, firm ones, ones from two feet off the edge, six feet in short grass, six feet in deep grass, six feet off a bald spot, six feet from a divot or hole, opposite handed beside a tree, landing on a downhill slope, landing on an uphill slope, sloppy-wet lies and so on and so forth.

One day last fall we had a surprise - an eight inch

snowfall (my golf course lies fifty miles from the Rocky Mountains)! On the third day after the snow, the putting green was the only snow-free area. The course was closed. The pro shop was locked. But it was a beautiful day and a sunny afternoon, so I was out practicing. After I had practiced for a while, another golfer appeared. He started chipping. After he had hit no more than ten shots, he remarked how boring it was! Out comes the putter and the guy hits about twenty putts. Boring? You bet! Two minutes later he says he's going home to watch TV. He cusses the snow and leaves. Me - I shrug my shoulders, continue putting, thinking I'm in heaven. There have to be at least 200 to 300 challenges around our putting green!!

Variation in practice

Harris* indicates that individual sports such as golf are more conducive to imagery practice because they are less complex. She stresses variation in practice as well, encouraging us to practice all kinds of options, to imagine situations and to imagine competing against a person better than ourselves. If I imagine Tom Watson success-fully hitting 9 of 10 from a deep grass buried lie, I would go after 4 of 10 and two days later go for 5 of 10. Sooner or later this practice pays off. One day, playing with our club professional, I had deep grass buried lie with the ball about ten inches under the top of the grass. I hit the shot one foot from the flag. I knew it was basically pure luck, but I had practiced that shot and had some image of what that swing was supposed to look like. So we say be "imagery-ready-Freddy"! Tom Watson has often said he was not particularly surprised when he holed out a deep grass cut wedge shot to win the U.S. Open in 1983. However, that shot has gone

Imagine situations and practice all kinds of options

---

*The reader might wish to obtain a copy of the sports psychology Athletes Guide, issued in 1984 by Dorothy Harris and Dr. Bette Harris (Longwood College, Farmville, Virginia), *Sports Psychology: Mental Skills for Physical People*. New York: Leisure Press, 1984. Leisure Press books are now available from Human Kinetics Publishers, Champaign-Urbana, Illinois (see bibliography for address).

down in history and millions of TV viewers were flabbergasted by that incredible shot! Now the professionals would be the first to say that amateurs rarely practice such a shot; and generally amateurs never would.

CHAPTER ONE
SUMMARY OF THE CHAPTER

- The left brain can improve the strategy in golf, the right brain can improve the swing itself, and the integrated brain allows all functions of brain and body to operate to lower golf scores. Incomplete notions are as harmful as helpful.

- The four types of imagery that are best utilized to assist with golf.

- The standards that can be used to develop imagery are carefully outlined. Direct improvement can result.

- How the golfer can use the brain and develop Tactics *Imagexercise©* to improve golf scores are introduced.

- The eleven key purposes for Golf *Imagexercise©* are clearly explained.

- Sport psychologists and the sciences they develop are explained. Many positive results are illustrated.

- Mental practice research proves the applicability of imagery to golf.

- The reasons that imagery can develop the golfer, their scores and their skills are given.

- Personality and imagery is detailed.

- The qualities of strong imagers and the common pitfalls in attempted usage of imagery are compared for the reader.

Chapter 2:
Imagery and Mental Skills as used by Professional Golfers

Objective:

The Chapter is based on what is known to be applied by PGA Tour professionals, LPGA professionals and golf instructors; some information from sport scientists and sport psychologists is also incorporated; the evidence of mushrooming growth of imagery is reviewed, the present status of imagery is outlined; advice to amateurs is presented; golf as a precision sport is reviewed; the historial aspect and how golfers such as Ben Hogan and others used and taught themselves imagery and other "mirror" skills; the author analyzes the best mental golfer of all time - Jack Nicklaus; to no rush-rush and the "coming attraction" notions are introduced.

Outstanding golf professionals have mentioned imagery for golf improvement in the books and articles they have written.

For example, when Grantland Rice ranked the five greatest putters of all time as Walter J. Travis, Jerry Travers, Bob Jones, Walter Hagen and Horton Smith, it was Horton Smith who wrote about imagery as a tactic for better putting and dealing with hills, rolls and plateaus on the greens.

He mentioned that it was the distance factor that made you decide if you should go for the one putt or settle for a two putt. With imagery technology you attempt to hit each putt so it will end up in the hole.

Horton Smith putting imagery

Jack Nicklaus saw the use of imagery as applying to both strategy and technique or ball striking, and discussed several aspects of imagery in his books.

Johnny Miller:
Imagery and Pure Golf

An even greater stress on imagery among golf professionals was indicated by Johnny Miller in his outstanding book on golf titled *Pure Golf.* Miller developed many different applications of golf imagery in his golf and gave advice to developing golfers.

Sylvia Bertoluccini credits imagery as the main reason for victory in a 1983 Tournament on the LPGA Tour. She said that she felt little mental stress because she had played the golf course eleven times on the evening prior to her final round by the medium of *Tactics Imagery* exercises. During her final round, she capitalized on the imagery application and easily controlled her mental game and won the tournament.

Mental Golf Movement:
A Bright Future From the 1984 Explosion

In 1984, the utilization of mental golf and particularly image golf received almost repeated application on the PGA and the LPGA Professional Tour.

Although there is a natural inclination to be somewhat secretive about the specifics there is enough evidence in the printed word and through interviews to be sure about such a statement. Some golf authorities move the date back to 1980 when mental golf and mental sport received an added boost. The boost came from Tim Gallwey's book (2) which most tennis players and some golfers read between 1977 and 1980. *Inner Tennis* rapidly became the most widely read book of its type. Other books were of equal importance and golf instructors and coaches (and golf professionals) absorbed more mental notions from these sources. Maxwell Maltz' *Psycho Cybernetics* and Norman Vincent Peale's *The*

Power of Positive Thinking were the main books coming out of the 60s.

Many ideas emerged, but a thread of visualization/imagery soon became a constant in the sports science literature. Relaxation theories were to go along with imagery and mental golf and Jacobsen's (Edmund) *Progressive Relaxation* became a popular and usable system in physical education and in fitness classes.

The National Golf Foundation of the U.S.A. and Its Role

About this time the National Golf Foundation of the PGA, centered in Florida, with consultants spread throughout America, did an excellent job of flogging the ideas of mental golf and golf instructional methods.

The National Golf Foundation did the golfers of the world and the Professional Tour a huge favor when it "discovered" a young caddy and psychologist by the name of Ed Grant from the University of Arizona. Grant was a self-taught golfer and a Tour caddy who found that contemporary writers did not discuss the mental aspects of golf to any degree and did not relate golf to brain function and enhancement. Joanne Winter, an LPGA (USA) Teacher of the Year is credited with making this "discovery" for the Golf Foundation.

Ed Grant took three years to put together a set of training materials on the basic ideas of subconscious golf. The NGF picked up the notion and several of its golf education sessions included Grant's talk. Materials were developed in both written and cassette tape format. The role of the subconscious brain, self-image, self talk and the comfort "zone" were explained. Most golfers could not handle getting out of their comfort "zone" or the idea of scoring lower than usual in their golf.

Ed Grant: Caddie and psychologist

Although not highly marketed, the NGF did its job of spreading Grant's gospel among several thousand PGA affiliated golf professionals, university and college golf instructors and coaches.

Grant had worked with two educational psychologists by the names of Bill Cole and Fred Mills of EDGE Inc. of Tempe, Arizona.

More Unexpected Help in Mental Golf for Professionals

Professional golfers, in the meantime, were beginning to reap some significant mental golf ideas from another unexpected source. Throughout the late 1950s and 1960s and later, young bright former athletes were taking graduate courses in tests and measurements and other university courses that included the earliest applications of sport psychologist ideas.

This movement lead to the development of sport psychologists as specialists, some of whom were former golfers and even certified golf professionals.

Rotella: Watson connection

Soon these sport psychologists started to work with Tour professionals and other athletes. In 1984, one such specialist received a great amount of recognition in the popular press of golf. Bob Rotella, a sport psychologist from the University of Virginia and a former golf professional, worked with Denis Watson, a relatively unknown Tour professional who had struggled for three years on Tour. Watson had enlisted the help of Rotella to go along with David Leadbetter, his swing mechanics instructor.

By working to improve Watson's swing, alignment and system of aiming, the two instructors, in effect, combined to instill confidence in their golfer.

Denis Watson

In the last six months of 1984, Watson played a string of amazing tournament performances that brought his yearly earnings to over $400,000 with accompanying benefits. Bob Rotella had used imagery and other sport psychology techniques in a program which resulted in Watson playing with supreme confidence. Watson and Mark O'Meara staged a dramatic battle for Player of the Year honors that year.

Ben Hogan: Coming Attraction Imagery

Despite the seeming added emphasis of the mental golf and imagery movement in recent times, there were strong golf success stories and successful mental golfers prior to our technical sport times. Successful "mental golf" was simply less common and was not subject to publicity and discussion as it is at present.

Ben Hogan won sixty-two tournaments, primarily between 1946 and 1953. He won the US Open three times and in 1953 was both US Open and British Open Champion. Born in 1912, he became a professional golfer at the age of seventeen. Only Jack Nicklaus and Sam Snead among men surpassed Hogan's record for number of victories. Kathy Whitworth is now the all time leader in this category.

Ben Hogan

Hogan became a golf legend and a review of his learning techniques and his game organization reveals a thread of imagery/visualization throughout. It is said that he was a golf legend in the 1950s because of his winning record and machine-like practice and game skills. Not only that but he was relatively small in stature and had basically taught himself the game. He suffered a near fatal car accident outside of Fort Worth, Texas in 1949, yet lived to win major tournaments again. A movie, *Follow The Sun*, immortalized the man.

Hogan and Imagery

For precise striking of the golf ball, Hogan depended on the precision duplication of swing positions that he had memorized. He did this in a number of unique ways. He is known to have used the following procedures.

In the first place he was a caddy. As caddy to Ed Stewart, a fine amateur at the Glen Garden Club, Hogan started memorizing swing details. He developed clear images of his golfer's swing and would compare his own swing to this model.

Hogan was able to recall and duplicate with great precision. Ed Stewart was a working man who did not golf a lot and Hogan said this gave him time to develop his own swing. Integration of imagery to the actual swing seemed to require a few days as Hogan found out.

Soon Hogan noticed swing details such as his left knee shooting straight out rather than folding in nicely. In a similar way he studied the whole swing. Hogan was known to have used up his parents small lawn with his practice. The lawns in this neighborhood were separated by hedges so young Ben would make his trips to the grocery store by hitting shots to the lawns as he travelled back and forth.

Johnny Revolta

When Hogan joined the professional tournament circuit in 1932, he soon came across Johnny Revolta, the premier short game player of the day. Revolta used the "waggle" (an abbreviated pre-swing club movement). Imagery generation came about with the waggle or the pre-hit club movement that Revolta used. Revolta had a large catalogue of "waggles" and they were each a different "coming attraction" of the shot to follow. Hogan described waggles such as those for a sort pop-up shot over the bunker to the green as a "waggle with sharp, staccato, jabby strokes" which Hogan called the *coming attraction* of the stroke to follow. Young Hogan really got into the waggle and the mental preview of the shot to follow.

The waggle and imagery

When Revolta had a shot to a slippery (downhill) point on the green, his waggle was "little pencil stroke waggles that seemed to be all fingertips." Hogan soon developed a large number of coming attraction images with accompanying club movements. In the modern technology of golf, we call this *preprogramming*. *Preprogramming* applies particularly to the putter, the wedge and the chip shot clubs. Another famous Texan golfer, Ben Crenshaw, advocates preprograming! However, most modern golfers preprogram and call it muscle memory. Imagery clarifies preprograming or shows you the exact way. All good putting and wedge play is based on effective preprograming of the backswing.

For Revolta and Hogan the coming attractions were duplicates of the real stroke but in miniature. Hogan clearly understood the role of the brain in golf. He provided his right brain or integrator swing selector brain with images that suggested total golf actions or "wholes."

Johnny Revolta taught golf at Rancho Mirage in Palm Springs, California a few years ago and the hands that showed Hogan the waggles back in the 30s are as huge and powerful and as "soft touch" as any golf hands you might hope to see (golf hands are special looking). The author simply marvelled at Revolta and his hands when he took in some Revolta advice a few years ago.

Midway through 1930, Hogan learned and "got" the correct hip turn. This time he committed it to image-memory after studying newsreel movies of the best golfers in action.

Hogan and the Swing Plane for Imagery

Somewhat later, Hogan grasped his clearest vision and version of the swing plane itself and its relation to hip and shoulder movement. Hogan was pleased with this development. As caddies in the 1950s we were advised to "groove our swing planes" (that is, swing so many times in the correct plane that we would be able to recall "it" automatically when golfing - lower scores among "grooved" swing plane golfers were common). Hogan used imagery and visual memory incessantly with swing plane and is known to have studied his backswing via full length mirrors in the motel rooms he used at tournaments. His reason for using mirrors was to memorize swing details so that he could "instinctively swing back the same way time after time." Here Hogan was telling golfers, in different terms, to know your swing well through vivid, controlled and repeated imagery. He was, as Tom Watson is, a student of repetition and accuracy of the stored image.

Hogan's "learning" of the golf swing seemed to bear real fruit in 1946. Now he enjoyed years of increasing success. He singles out 1946 as the year he finally became self-confident. Prior to that he had not lost feelings of self-doubt, or the feeling that he could lose it all swing wise, at any time. Hogan gave a clear reason for this change. It is related to imagery. Hogan said he simply stopped the idea of trying to do a great many things too perfectly. Instead he decided that all he needed to do was to groove the fundamental movements and he stated that there were not too many of them. Moreover,

Swing plane as imagery

Hogan began to believe (6) that the fundamental movements in golf not only were limited in number, but also were controllable.

Hogan's golfing friends told him to relax and trust his "grooved swing."

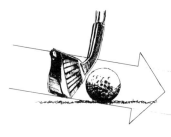

Simplifying the Need for Image Quantity

Once a golfer reaches a certain level of confidence, he requires less quantity in the way of images and a simplified and reduced storage capacity for images. For example, as indicated previously, a vivid picture of the front shoulder turning and being flexible and level may be all that is required. To the experienced golfer this *one* image stands for many other aspects of their swing.

From an imagery point of view this means less images overall to store in the brain and a greater possibility of vivid controlled imagery.

We are also lead to one other definite advantage if we decide to follow Hogan's conclusion about keeping the golf swing simple. In addition to fewer images ("coming attractions") there would be more confidence on the golf course, and more time for strategy and tenacity to develop in the golfer's game.

Further along in Ben Hogan's famous *Sports Illustrated* issues of *The Modern Fundamentals of Golf*, he indicated such advantages. Apparently Hogan thought he could play creditable golf when not at his very best, especially within the grind of tournament after tournament!!

Confidence and consistency

A new and stable golf consistency can be based upon the notion that the more you can trust your swing to memory (images stored at the creative subconscious level) the more time you can spend managing your game on and off the golf course. Hogan's controllable fundamentals numbered eight in all and formed a chain of action, including the waggle which allowed proper timing and follow through. The phases of the chain were subject to imagery.

It appears that *Benjamin William Hogan* was one of the professional greats who truly used and believed in mental imagery (his own version to be sure!). It does not appear that he had trouble at all with the vivid recallable images that he used from his caddying days onward.

Recovery from injury was also within Hogan's capabilities. Severe trauma recovery associated with injury is becoming more and more to do with strong will via strong images of life and life-skills. Hogan's golf skill was strongly aligned with mental golf and in light of his 1949 car accident, it appears that months of immobilized bed care cannot prevent a mentally active patient from "exercising" muscle motor memory through excitation of the central nervous system.

Chemically based brain function

This chemically based "brain-miracle" may be the same reason that a pilot taken prisoner for three years kept his sanity and desire to excel at golf intact through imagery recall and golf game rehearsals and shot a 75 the first time out. The pilot mentally duplicated a five hour golf game complete with warm-up, socializing and food breaks while he spent his days in prison. Perhaps Hogan did the same thing.

Obtain an original issue copy of *Sports Illustrated*'s "revolution in teaching," *The Modern Fundamentals of Golf*, by Ben Hogan with Herbert Warren Wind. It contains unbelievable illustrations by Anthony Ravielli (illustrator, artist). The five-part series appeared in March and April 1957. Try a used book store. If you do not want the collector's original, the series as a book has recently been re-issued by *Golf Digest* book services.

Examples of Imagery by the Golf Professionals

As baseball players are advised to use an image of a pitched ball that looks larger than a real ball, so too are golfers advised to see a larger hole. Since the brain does not reject a "fantasized" image, a larger golf hole than 4-1/4" is excellent to utilize. Jack Fleck, who upset Hogan in the 1955 U.S. Open, reported that from the 5th hole on in the final round the hole started looking as big as a

Imagery of enlarged golf cup builds confidence

washtub. He became convinced he could not miss and that is exactly what happened. He did not question his image, he just kept it and trusted it.

In reality a golf hole doubled in size to 8-1/2″ may look like a "small quarry hole" but in the British scientific experiments in golf, the conclusion was that it made little difference in reducing an eighteen hole golf score (some six shots was all). But, under imagery conditions the drop in score from a non-imagery trial may have been much more substantial!!! Apparently, if the hole is really large the typical golfer gets a little careless and misses the six footers regardless. A hole that is "larger" only in one's mind is different. Such an image simply builds confidence and assists recollection of stored muscle memory in the brain. This assures a good putt stroke and better putting.

My belief is that a good mental golfer would shoot in the 60s most of the time if the hole was 8-1/2″. The current Professional record for the low Tour competitive score (the 59 by Al Geiberger) would soon disappear, since that record would likely be broken any time.

A Key Image for a Slow Paced Backswing in Golf

Perhaps the most common swing image among Tour professionals is that of a slowly paced backswing. Bobby Jones used to say that it is not possible to swing too slowly and the slow take away and leisurely hands assure a full "turn." Tom Watson and Nancy Lopez claim that it is important to be able to see the clubhead move away at a speed that can be "followed" visually and they have both cultivated such a swing. The image selected for this should be narrowed down to one favorite one by the golfer. Certainly sitting near Nancy Lopez's father as she hits several hundred practice balls is a learning experience which reinforces such an image notion. Her father knows a lot about how Lopez should be swinging a golf club.

Hall Sutton, during a streak of particularly hot golf in 1983, said that he concentrated on smoothness and deliberateness (i.e., slowness in the

Tom Watson
Nancy Lopez
Hal Sutton

execution of movements in golf) on all of his golf shots. He tried to "accelerate through the ball." Sutton won with this approach.

Concentrate on smoothness and deliberateness in golf shots

One great *Technique Imagexercise*© is to utilize humming or even a low whistle as you program the acceleration of your practice swing. It greatly reduces your tendency to "over think" and also suggests a relaxed golf swing. Use the same "slow to faster" tune and your creative subconscious will soon pick up your rhythmical cues. Sony "walkman" cassette tape playback units have been successfully used by a few golfers "brave" enough to try them on the professional Tour (for example, Dick Zokal and others). By doing so, you will no longer require this aid as it becomes programmed in your brain. A suggestion would be to use a walkman on the putting green for a rhythmical putt motion since the "rhythm" muscle memory will likely stay with you on the golf course. If you cue your swing with a hum or whistle, you will strike the ball well for most of your round. On the other hand, we ask our Junior development program golfers at our club not to use the walkman for zombie-like punk rock or other non-golf compatible music.

Other Images Used by Professionals

Prior to placing the feet in a consistent pre-shot swing routine, almost all Tour professionals visualize the flight of the ball, with some of them taking the trouble and time to "watch" the ball "land" and "roll to a stop." After the right foot is set, the club and body is squared and set and the left foot is then placed (the opposite for left handers). Imagery continues briefly during which the golfer sees the "swing" required to make the imagined shot. For an experienced golfer who has a good tempo and flow of energy started this last image might be of one key specific aspect such as seeing "slow hands," seeing "head position," or seeing a "T square and arrowhead" driving through the ball or even a "hands behind the left ear follow through."

Visualize the flight of the ball

Perseverence and Professional Versus Amateur Differences

When Tom Watson was a high school football player in Kansas, he showed an athletic skill and life skill commonly labelled as *Perseverence*. Falling behind 7-21 at half time in a key high school game did little to discourage Watson, as he and his team came back with a thirty-five yard winning touchdown pass near the end of the game. Tenacity *Imagexercise©* as detailed in this book has enormous impact on a good golf score, particularly during the last six holes, when most golfers "fall asleep" or do some mental daisy picking.

Most Tour professionals seem to agree that the biggest difference between a Tour player and a low handicap amateur is that the bad shots are not as bad by the Tour player. This suggests careful preparation through imagery, prior practice and overall experience. Greg Norman, the Australian professional, believes that the short game may be sharper and that both the physical and mental game are "honed" by U.S. PGA competition. Norman will not give away his mental game "secrets" but he seems to think that Tour players are good at mental golf. Jack Nicklaus still feels that patience (key to mental and physical consistency) is the biggest single factor in determining winners and losers in golf - at all levels.

"Bad shots" not as bad among Tour professionals

Psyched Up Approach by the Professional Golfer

The psyched up approach prevalent in sports such as football appears to be limited in use by professional golfers. The imagery review stage will simply not have time to occur if the golfer is still angry from the last shot. Sometimes an upset golfer "cranks" out his next drive further than usual, but it is more likely that he finds trouble with such a "psyched up" shot. A golf course seems to have innumerable ways of taking strokes off a golfer. Jay Haas, a young Tour professional, has an uncle who is Bob Goalby, the 1968 Masters champion. Haas

Jay Haas

has learned a lot from his uncle including learning not to be hot-tempered as his uncle was in his earlier playing days.

Haas contrasted the ability to forget bad shots quickly with the approach that helps some people - that of getting charged up. Charged up is an effective approach if the golfer can keep the approach for long periods of time. The *Imagexercise©* is of the other approach, although many sports psychologists stress that lingering too long over any skill in sport can be ineffective due to tension build-up. Ken Venturi agrees with this notion. Despite this, the lingering anger and visualization of a bad shot has to be replaced with a well-timed, positive *Imagexercise©* approach. Pre-rehearsed imagexercises are excellent for "anger" situations because the golfer has a set routine involving imagery. Allowing imagery to intervene allows time to cool down that anger and save a disaster or two. However, learning is required and quite a lot of effort is involved in becoming a great imagery golfer. Jay Haas stresses patience.

Lingering anger and visualization of a bad shot must be replaced with a well timed, positive imagexercise approach

Most golfers on Tour have to accept a purpose for their lives and a patience that overrides feelings that they *have to succeed*. The added pressure of this attitude is often too much to cope with in a profession that is already pressure-prone. A surprising number have stressed that easing-off on themselves has led to vast improvement. Jocelyne Bourassa, a former LPGA Tour player, stated this well when she said in an interview that "once I am able to get a better picture of who I am and where I'm going I'll be able to be singing out on Tour once again." This professional attitude is just as necessary for the amateur golfer. The vast majority of amateurs appear less than realistic about their golf. Good tactics are a very reasonable way for the amateur golfer to seek improvement, especially if they are unrealistic about their swing potential. Later on, they can become more realistic about the swing, its potential and its problems.

Bourassa and "professional" attitude

Negative Imagery
Among the Tour Players

Kathy Hite

Kathy Hite is a Tour player who understands that a negative thought can cause a negative image that an active creative subconscious can turn into a bad golf shot. She was once on her way to a tournament record 65 when an inexperienced caddy shocked her by asking what would happen if she hit one into the water on the 12th hole.

After asking her caddy to never talk that way again, she managed to "refocus" her mind's eye on a positive image before teeing off. She almost hit the hole and made birdie.

The subconscious is neither rational nor evaluative! If the last mind message you sent to it is what will happen if you hit the water, you will likely hit into the water. This example suggests that even caddies must be aware of psychology in sport. If you are saving an old ball for water shots you will have a pretty difficult time striking a shot other than the one you are suggesting. *Suggestion* is the basis of a whole variety of psych-out ploys and effects in golf. For many golfers, there is too much time to think in golf. The extra time before you get your chance to hit must be used positively. That is why pre-rehearsal imagery tactics are vital to our three and one-half hour minimum game. Worse yet is the occasional golfer's five hour game during which all kinds of horrific negative image time exists.

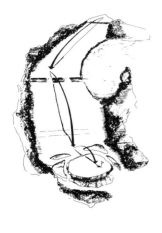

Precision Machines

There are many painful and poignant examples of lack of success on the Professional Golf Tour. John Harris, a former All American golfer from Minnesota, once told a reporter that the one thing that struck him most as he tried for success on Tour was the "almost inhuman" quality of the golfer's machine-like swings and games. They were likened to precision machines, some small, some big but all with precision games. *But the most important thing he said was something else! The* St. Paul Pioneer Press reported that he also said,

"The Thinkers who can control their minds rise to the top. They can concentrate and they know when and how to relax."

He should have expected the precision. Although he called it a cold ruthless business, with no time for friendship, that probably is not true either. I have noticed quite some camaraderie and good natured remarks on the practice tee and the putting green at Tour tournaments.

Mind Control, Concentration and Relaxation

These three skills are all worthy of time and effort by golfers at any level. They portray very closely the skills that we hope you initiate or develop in reading and exercising imagery from this book. Mental skills and relaxation skills become more important than striking skills. Lots of golfers would be quite happy to get to this stage in golf development. Most sport science authorities suggest that athletes like you should learn relaxation skills and mental skills. Learn these skills as early as you learn ball striking skills. Since this will be the future way of learning sport you might as well do it in the here and now!!!

Golf Professionals Ranked as Poor Visualizers

Dr. Craig Farnsworth, a sports vision consultant and member of the American Optometric Association, spoke recently at both the Los Angeles Pre-Olympic Scientific Congress and at a Sport Vision Conference in Calgary, Alberta, Canada. His lab is located in Lakewood, Colorado and his recent visual and visualization improvement sessions included Tour players as well as a variety of other "tracking skill athletes." It is his opinion, based on recent work with golf professionals, that less than 10 percent of them successfully use a program of mental imagery in their golf. The golfers' opinions are that their images are technically inaccurate. They have great difficulty using visual memory just

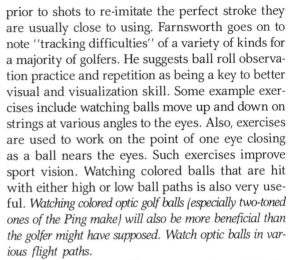

Ball roll observation practice and repetition: Key to better visual and visualization skill

Role of optic golf balls

prior to shots to re-imitate the perfect stroke they are usually close to using. Farnsworth goes on to note "tracking difficulties" of a variety of kinds for a majority of golfers. He suggests ball roll observation practice and repetition as being a key to better visual and visualization skill. Some example exercises include watching balls move up and down on strings at various angles to the eyes. Also, exercises are used to work on the point of one eye closing as a ball nears the eyes. Such exercises improve sport vision. Watching colored balls that are hit with either high or low ball paths is also very useful. *Watching colored optic golf balls (especially two-toned ones of the Ping make) will also be more beneficial than the golfer might have supposed. Watch optic balls in various flight paths.*

Due to this, some golf camps are using optic balls in an effort to assure minimal ball flight watching abilities. *Practice with optic golf balls every chance you get and watch the ball flight path from the side as well as from behind the ball.*

Can Any Golfer Improve Visual Skills for Golf and Ball Tracking?

If golf professionals are not capable of *Imagexercise©*, then why should you be? The answer is: Let us take the position or opinion that anyone can improve these skills given practice and visual ability or potential. It does so happen that you will have to build up a "bank" of images and you will have to become more visual than verbal. However, so does everyone else in sport. *We* are all very verbal and not very visual. About 75 percent of improving your visual skills is changing your environment around you so that you are constantly

in a more visually demanding environment. When you think about it, that is not difficult to arrange although it will require persistence to perfect. About 75 percent of eliminating the verbal overload in golf is in developing a bank of images that mean a lot to you; that you see very well; and that you believe in 101 percent of the time! You can apply them and they will motivate you.

If you combine this book and its exercises with

three or four good videotapes you are on your way to becoming an "out of sight" golfer!!

Videotapes such as the new golf videotapes supply you with many swing demonstrations as a resource to develop your images. Recommended videotapes are found in the major North American golf magazines. The "Play your best golf" videotapes from Caravett Home Entertainment are good examples featuring top PGA professionals, instructors from the PGA, *Golf Digest* Teachers of the Year in the LPGA, University of Alabama and Duke University golf coaches.

Golf videos and the visual environment

Your image skills and confidence can be a well-kept secret if you want - just like Greg Norman, the "Great White Shark" whose mental skills are his secrets!! I agree with Greg Norman that there are some application secrets.

Greg Norman

It is my observation and that of other golf instructors that most occasional and regular golfers are far too burdened with swing theories that often exacerbate their swing problems. By trying to apply more than one swing theory you are simply "diluting" the effectiveness of some key notions of another theory. It is a sport cliche that is as old as the hills and as true as the heavens to "do what you do well" and to use the *Kiss* principle of "keep it simple silly."

Suggestion and Altered Perception of Time

Imagery can often be cued in or used by suggesting a "slowing down." Tour players cultivate this by control of swing speed on the practice fairway. However, some professional players contend that a slow leisurely pace of activities prior to arriving for practice the day of an important tournament serves as a powerful *suggestion*. Walter Hagen was considered to be an advocate of being "leisurely." He paced his morning activities such as shaving, having breakfast and travelling to the site of competition. George Knudson, a successful Tour player of the 1970s starts "cooling it" the night before. Cary Middlecoff suggests music of a soft rhythmical type to enhance his swing pace.

**Patty Sheehan
and daily living habits**

**Michael Murphy
and psychic sport**

No rush-rush

Patty Sheehan stresses regular life habits and patterns of daily living so that she always has the "feeling" of organization in her life. She never feels hurried. All such factors suggest an image or visualization of patience. Patience leads to consistency. Patience also breeds *Time Management* which suggests consistency. Michael Murphy, author of *The Psychic Side of Sport*, has written extensively about altered perception of time, time distortion, and how athletes obtain information through telepathy, ESP and precognition. Relative to the Tour players slowing their pace and controlling swing speed, he has mentioned that "it is exciting to consider that even though the passage of time has not actually slowed down, nevertheless the fact that it feels as if it has apparently enables the athlete to accomplish more, just as he would if in fact he did have more time, more amplitude."

Businessmen and executive or professional ladies may have a difficult time slowing their pace prior to a golf game. For this purpose we have developed a unique *Imagexercise©* called the *No Rush-Rush* which has a reasonable chance of slowing down a golf swing by the time you tee off. It utilizes a combination of preparation completed the evening before and a ninety second slow down drill on the putting green to be done as "you rush to the first tee." See page 50 in Chapter 3.

Imagery and Athletic and Golf Enhancement

Another aspect of the enhancement of golf performance was reported by Charles Hogan and an associate in issues of *Golf Magazine* in late 1984 and early 1985.

At the same time and in the same place, two golf imagery "happenings" occurred in Eugene, Oregon. In July 1984, a research paper confirming that imagery worked effectively with occasional golfers was read at the Eugene Sports Congress. In the early summer of 1984, also in Eugene, a golf professional and a scientist developed what they called "an image *generator*" and coupled it with an intensive week-long imagery program. The imagery program was accompanied by relaxation sessions and a "truck load of positives" as Ray Floyd was later to describe it. As a result of such an imagery program (called Sport Enhancement) several professional Tour players, after working with Mr. Hogan and his associate, Dale VanDalsem, exhibited extreme performance improvement. Peter Jacobsen is reported to have spent four days on "enhancement" and next week won the Colonial Invitational, his first Tour victory since 1980. Jacobsen had been described as a Tour player of "incredible motivation, physical talent and discipline, *and* with not a clue on how to get a handle on the mental side of the game." Ray Floyd spent a week on Enhancement in August 1984 and came out of it with a positive attitude and what was described as a superior ability to create vivid images. Floyd led the PGA golf tournament after his image enhancement experience.

Of more importance to amateurs was the prediction by the "Enhancement developers" that an 8-10 handicapper such as George Peper (a golf writer with *Golf Magazine*) might be able to play as a 1-4 handicap for the rest of his golf life, after a week of such enhancement. In fact, George Peper was very pleased with his next seven golf games after reading about visualization and simply having a determination to visualize every shot. Peper shot seven games of 80 and below and had one 73 at his home golf course after his "visualization" experience. Mr. Peper has called the developers of enhancement "Voodoo Doctors," but they are not that at all!!

George Peper

They have simply seen the connection and realized that golfers have not developed their sensorial pathways and their visual skills to a degree that matches the golfer's need in this area. They help the golfer develop a set of images and belief that these images can be trusted.

To a large extent, we believe that a carefully developed and well thought out program of imagery development brings on the same potential for success as reported above. Being somewhat cautious

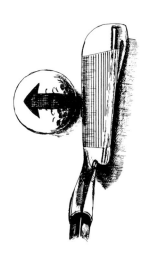

Internalizing a golf image system

Learning to trust your images is harder than acquiring the images themselves

about the potential of Imagery is wise, if for no other reason than that Imagery skills are somewhat harder to come by and "internalize" than some proponents would have you believe. To internalize an image golf system means to trust it in competitive circumstances. The belief that your images can be trusted may be harder to acquire than the images themselves.

This book, properly studied, will help you see the potential that exists and may help you internalize your belief in the *Imagexercise©* system.

As a result, your golf scores should be lowered and consistent when you golf on a regular basis.

CHAPTER TWO
SUMMARY OF THE CHAPTER

This chapter summary will take the form of a list of "mental characteristics" in golf. For the most part such characteristics have been mentioned by those rated as "golf greats" when they have discussed other golf champions. In addition, sport scientists have studied the same characteristics and their input has been added. Finally, based on recent evidence (post 1980) a characteristic labelled "highly developed mental skill" has been added. It is composed of the three-way skill of mental imagery, relaxation and concentration. Concentration varies with each athlete but in general it is the ability to stay on task and on skill despite distracting circumstances.

The *characteristics* listed on the following pages are ranked in order of importance only for the first six characteristics. A definition is given and a top exponent among male golfers is named. The greats among LPGA women need to be the subject of a separate study.

The second aspect of the rating is by input by the "greats" themselves. Other writers have provided ratings in one form or another.

Characteristics

1. Highly Developed Mental Skills

Definition:
Concentration and confidence stemming from imagery skills, relaxation and golf background.

Exponent:
Jack Nicklaus, Ben Hogan, Tom Watson, Johnny Miller. Relaxation skills were not nearly as evident in earlier career.

2. Not Particularly Physically Gifted

Definition:
A ''grinder'' in sports parlance, ability to maximize god-given talents.

Exponent:
Walter Hagen, Ben Hogan, Henry Cotton, Bobby Locke, Gary Player, Cary Middlecoff and Jack Nicklaus.

3. Desire to Excel

Definition:
A drive or motivation to narrow the gap between best and worst shots in golf.

Exponent:
Walter Hagen, Ben Hogan, Henry Cotton, Bobby Locke, Cary Middlecoff, Lee Trevino, Gary Player, Tom Watson and Jack Nicklaus.

4. Competitive Drive

Definition:
Competition brings out the best in them.

Exponent:
Harry Vardon, Walter Hagen, Gene Sarazen, Bob Jones and Arnold Palmer.

5. Belief that Mind is More Important than Method

Definition:
Constant attention to mental aspects of golf.

Exponent:
Ben Hogan, Jack Nicklaus, Henry Cotton, Tom Watson.

6. Belief in Perfectionism

Definition:
Keyed in to perfectionism.

Exponent:
Ben Hogan, Jack Nicklaus, Cary Middlecoff and Byron Nelson.

7. Emotional Stability

Definition:
Tournament golf not so important that it is life itself.

Exponent:
Harry Vardon, Walter Hagen, Bob Jones, Johnny Miller, and Tom Weiskopf.

8. Placidness*

Definition:
Unperturbable, not apathetic; in golf it seems to mean patience.

Exponent:
Harry Vardon, Julius Boros, Sev Ballesteros and Jack Nicklaus.

9. Belief in Great Physical Attributes

Definition:
Expressed or internalized belief that golf is an athletic gift.

Exponent:
Bob Jones, Sam Snead and Tom Weiskopf.

10. Extraordinary Touch

Definition:
Short game and putting excellence.

Exponent:
Arnold Palmer, Bill Casper, Bobby Locke, Tom Watson and Bob Murphy.

---

* Number 8 not ranked but in random order.

11. Willpower

Definition:
Desire to excel; attacking; "willing" the ball into the hole. Separates the good and the great.

Exponent:
Arnold Palmer.

These characteristics of the Tour professionals tend to point to one golfer, Jack Nicklaus, who commands universal acceptance from his peers.

Young Hal Sutton expressed it very well in 1981 when he remarked that Nicklaus is the man I admire "he is so poised. He has that look of a winner in his eyes."

(*Golf Digest*, February 1981)

Chapter 3
Introduction to Imagexercise Golf

Objective:
Using visualization and imagery as an exercise in order to play low scoring golf; common golf problems and Imagexercise© *Golf; definition and use for* Imagexercise© *(IE); golfers' use of log books and journals to improve their golf; setting up for permanent use and evaluating the benefits.*

Common Problems for Imagexercise© Golf

The Set Pre-Shot Routine

Most golfers play much better when they have established a set pre-shot routine as they play a golf stroke. In fact, most golf instructors believe that the routine should be augmented with various *Imagexercises©* such as those that follow and that are noted above.

Images Required

- An aim-line IE (1)
- A shot-shape IE (2)
- Ball landing behavior IE (3)
- Swing rhythm (4)
- Swing technique IE (5)

An aim-line IE (*Imagexercise©* or exercise of golf visualization) is an imaginary line from the ball past a near marker such as an old divot, broken tee or

"Accelerate through the ball"

cigarette butt, and on to the target. A shot-shape image, a ball landing behavior image and a swing rhythm image are the key areas in addition to the image of the swing itself. Normally a golfer uses an image for each part of the pre-shot routine.

The swing rhythm IE is an internal image (within your body) just as the feel for the swing is. The external images that you use are for imitating swing rehearsals or other swing models which arise from outside you.

See an image of such a routine and your golf will start exhibiting precision. Repeat your routine program on each shot no matter how short or easy you think it is. Each shot counts the same as any other shot. Learn the procedure mentioned above and make it a routine. Also keep another general idea in mind. If you want an evenly paced motion, imagine a child swinging on a swing and imitate how the swing goes back, pauses and then returns with a little extras surge of speed. You can even whisper the message to your subconscious brain and your creative subconscious will like it and will repond very well. Notice that the child swinging motion suggests *Swing Tempo and Acceleration*. Numbers 1 to 5 in the diagram on the previous page comprise the imagery for a set pre-shot routine. Select one image for each part of the routine and try to repeat the routine prior to each shot. *Consistency* is the biggest factor in low scoring golf and this routine produces consistency.

General Swing Shape with Specific Cues

Imagexercise© should be used as your swing indoors in front of a mirror to develop swing precision and repeatability. As you exercise by swinging, use images to provide a reference. Your images should be of a set of swing pictures (or a videotape) suitable to your body build and natural swing features. It is recommended that five or six basic positions should be imaged. Johnny Miller has mentioned that as a seven-year-old, he hit balls in the basement of his house against a canvas as he compared his swing to the swings of Ben Hogan, Sam Snead and "Iron" Byron Nelson.

Images Required

Technique *Imagexercise©* for:

- Addressing the ball
- Top of backswing stretch
- Hands back down to belt level
- Impact
- Belt level past ball and high follow through

Earlier we mentioned, and now stress, how Ben Hogan stored coming attraction images for swing plane while he swung via mirrors in hotel rooms when he was on the professional golfers Tour. Before going out to the golf course, you should stress the above image and swing exercise just as Hogan did until you have a grooved swing.

Addressing the ball imagery

One-Half Swing or the Toe Up (1), Square (2), Toe Up Exercise (3)

A common swing feature, once you are beyond the introductory stage in golf, is the ability to square up the club face at impact with the golf ball. You may have noticed that if you turn over the wrists and the club face too soon you hit a bad hook-type shot. However, by using *Imagexercise©* to plant a firm and vivid picture of the correct arm-wrist and club movement in your subconscious, you will control any tendency to turn over "too soon."

Use the pictures above to develop an *Imagexercise©* for the toe up activity. The pictures show three key positions. Image each.

Image Required

Technique *Imagexercise©* for:

- Toe up "belt line"
- Club and hand position
- Hand and club "squared up" at impact
- Toe up at "belt line" after the hit

Attempt to feel and check your image for each of the three key positions as you swing your club.

The result of this key *Imagexercise©* is the squared up club face at impact. Combined with a slightly inside-out swing path (which is a normal swing path), this will result in a straight hit. Working the ball to the left or right can also be accomplished in this way.

The name one-half swing does not mean to swing only one-half a swing, but rather to "image check" your full swing at two swing positions or at the belt line going back and again at the belt line going forward. Notice that the back of your left hand is positioned nearly vertically through all of these swing positions.

This *Imagexercise©* is an example of a basic technique of the swing that can be learned and reinforced through exercise of your imagery.

Capturing Good Performance

Golf authorities agree that it is not enough to get a "good general feeling" for your swing. They suggest that you get the exact feeling interconnected to an *Imagexercise©* that stresses feel as a reminder of playing well.

Images Required

- Recapturing the "feeling and image of a swing" from prior good golf.

Feeling or Kinetics images

The feel that your swing gives you when you are playing well can come and go, so you should write a description of the feeling in a golf note book. A student golfer, for example, wrote of "how she changed her knuckle position in the grip and got a good drive with a feeling of complete follow through and high finish." This is an *Imagexercise©*

that received positive reinforcement during a golf game. Her swing improved because she could keep a key swing accomplishment for the future.

Regular golfers should "get on and keep on a roll" when playing well by stressing this dynamic, on-going use of imagery. Occasional golfers might also discover uses for this method. Capturing "good performance" uses both left brain and right brain; the left in analyzing several cues and the right in selecting and duplicating the whole swing. *Image is the Key!*

Commenting on the PGA National Academy of Golf for Juniors, Dr. Gary Wiren, former Educational Director of the PGA, noted that all the visiting Tour golf stars stress the following short list of fundamentals (PGA Annual):

1. Learn to make a *Swing* and know what it *Feels* like.
2. *Aim* your clubface, then your body.
3. *Square* the clubface while keeping the left wrist flat.

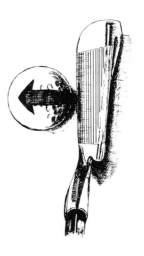

The *Imagexercise©* activities presented so far simply make it easier for the golfer to learn and to keep using these three principles. They are evident in the Tour professional and his/her swing and should be in the learner's swing and set-up or routine. The same type of routine for aiming the clubface and then the body that won over $400,000 for Denis Watson (in six months of 1984) is the same routine *all* golfers require. Watson and other Tour stars simply perfect their routines, perfect their swing feel and perfect their "square clubfaces"   **Denis Watson** at impact with the ball more than do regular golfers.

Imagexercise© will make it easier for you to remember and apply these principles and fundamentals.

A Few More Common Applications for *Imagexercise©*

It was predicted by *Golf Digest* staff in 1984 that serious golfers would understand their golf assets and liabilities in the future and that activities would be used to train parts of the body to work correctly. For example, a common "liability" for many golfers is created by rushing, both before and during a golf game.

Images Required

• See yourself as a "No Rush-Rush" golfer.

The no rush-rush

The "No rush-rush" is a form of *Imagexercise*© needed by almost all golfers at one time or another. Rushing to the first tee and striking a disastrous first drive sets a chain of "rushed actions" into motion. Our brain and the creative subconscious cannot cope with or fix such rushed actions. All of your "suggestions" just prior to teeing off are the patterns set into motion by your brain. These suggestions can be devastating to the golfer. The chain reaction that can be set up is just as if you have an "all-rush" messenger service to your brain.

Essentially, "trick" your subconscious as follows:

Even though you know that you are pressed for time to get to the golf course, do a lot of pre-imagery (and prepreparation). See that you already have yourself ready in many ways. Your shoes may be polished, your tees are in a neat, small bag instead of scattered throughout the bottom of a golf bag pocket and everything is picked out for the game. Phone ahead to the golf course to say you will be there, even if "on the fly" this time. Your subconscious brain will soon get the idea that you are organized and patient (*The two qualities you will need to play a low scoring golf game*). If you do not have the time to hit a few practice balls or some chips, go straight to the putting green on the way to the first tee, take out your putter and stand three feet from a hole and mentally and physically rehearse your "great controlled putting stroke." See the ball path and the ball fall into the exact middle of the hole a few times. Pick out the exact blade of grass, in the exact middle of the 4-1/4" cup and knock in a few one footers. If you have time, knock a few more one footers into the cup to show your subconscious how firmly and exactly you are "banging the ball" into the hole. After this sixty

Two qualities to play low-scoring golf

to ninety second drill, go behind the tee box and loosen up your shoulders and legs and physically take a few practice swings. *Now* step up to the tee with your subconscious completely unaware of how you had to hurry down the freeway to the golf course parking lot just a few minutes ago. This is one of the best *Tenacity* (mental toughness) *Imagexercise©* you can develop and it simply amounts to mind-control and being tough and demanding with your subconscious brain. Perhaps it is strange to say so, *but* you must communicate with your own brain in this regard. You must deliver the correct golf messages to your brain.

Slow to Faster Tempo

Use *Imagexercise©* for slow to faster swing speed (tempo) as follows and remember that all effective golf is based on excellent control of your personal swing tempo. Imagine a slowly but forcefully increasing sports car turbo-engined acceleration (try a fantasy Porsche Targa) or see a jet accelerate. While at your job for the last couple of hours, do all your work with totally controlled tempo. Swing your arms once in a while in a golf motion. Do a putt motion with great tempo and control. Finally, when driving to the golf course use the gas pedal and brake with particularly good acceleration/deceleration. Arrive early and do not hurry!

Images Required

- Develop a favorite set of slow to faster tempo *Imagexercise©*

An *Imagexercise©* for relating swing speed to the legs was done successfully by Johnny Miller with his son John Jr. when he had John visualize and use "soft knees." Soft knees relate to a soft swing of the arms. This image is used to interconnect two parts of the body to one swing idea. Another concept image he encouraged was of a "tiger about to swing." This top of the backswing image suggests a nice stretch action, with a tiny pause, and is very effective in the golf swing. Miller generally encouraged all kinds of images (and practice) for all kinds of variety shots and all kinds of trouble golf situations.

Glen Campbell, the singer-songwriter, was a 10 handicapper when he was in need of a fuller backswing (or more flexible shoulders). He developed a picture of himself getting all of his weight over to his right side before he started the swing back down. To practice this do an exercise we use with all golf classes. Swing to the top and temporarily lift up your front foot then set it down and continue the swing (as with all exercises, do not overdo this since the front foot should have a good feeling for the ground underneath it). The result of this for Glen Campbell was a better shoulder turn. A specific image was needed for this swing correction. Another *Imagexercise©* all golfers require to play to their potential is to see a picture of knowing how far your game can take you.

Glen Campbell

Knowing How Far Your Game Can Take You

Images Required

- *Imagexercise©* the idea that you know how far your game can take you.

If you go to watch the men play on the Tour, follow Jack Renner for a few holes. Usually he is dressed in light shades or greys, usually he is wearing a flat-top golf cap, usually he strikes the ball with incredible precision for all his tall, rather skinny appearance, and usually he almost seems to be saying to you, "I'm going to hit every shot as well as every other shot; I'm concentrating; I don't have great expectations, although I'm good enough to win."

Jack Renner's persistence wins

Jack Renner seems to be a persistent athletic-type. In fact, during an interview after Renner's first big win at *Westchester,* he said simply (before the last round), "I have no great expectation of winning this tournament. I'm just going around. I'm not hitting the ball well but I am concentrating well." After he won the tournament, he added, ''There are positives and negatives about winning. The positives are the money and knowing I can win. The negatives are that people are going to expect a great deal out of me. I'm not in the class of a Watson, a Weiskopf, or a Nicklaus. Maybe in five years I could be,'' (quoted in "Tour talk." John May. G.D., 1978). You may be interested to note that by 1985 Renner had accumulated $1,046 million in winnings. He had a first, second and third and $260,000 in one year.

My guess is that I play with a lot of golfers who do not have a realistic idea (or an image) of how far their game can take them. Renner is just the opposite. The unrealistic ones are usually former low handicappers who say they once "played well." Playing well can be an excruciatingly difficult level to acquire in golf. It is true that during the long hard grind to become a good competitive amateur player you must constantly reevaluate the goals and standards you are setting for your game. Normally you overestimate "how far your game can take you." This is the mental or tenacious aspect of golf. Failure to invoke a basic *Tenacity Imagexercise©* is wasteful of your time and is frustrating as well. This is such an important problem in athletics that in coach and physical education teacher development programs, there is a stress on coaches working with athletes, especially young and maturing athletes, so that these athletes are capable of dealing with themselves and this problem. They are taught to understand their athletic strengths and weaknesses. Young athletes' emotional outbursts of anger are tied to this basic tenet of athletic development.

Ways to Use *Imagexercise©*

A summary of the uses of *Imagexercise©* in golf follows:

1. *Use Imagexercise© to improve your swing.* Develop accurate mental pictures and then match your body movements to these golf positions. Narrow the images down to those that are best for your swing.

2. Use *Imagexercise©* to improve your tactics.

3. Use *Imagexercise©* to demand more of yourself on the golf course (we call it *Tenacity Imagexercise©*). For example, each time you step on the putting green and each time you go through a pre-shot routine you will have to be *thorough* and mentally demanding of yourself. Enjoy this special challenge in golf.

Self-efficacy becomes your strength of conviction in improving

4. Use *Imagexercise©* to build your confidence.

5. Use *Imagexercise©* to build your self-efficacy or strength of conviction that you can improve.

6. Use *Imagexercise©* to learn new skills such as difficult or uncommon golf shots or even trap shots. Prepare for almost all eventualities on the golf course.

7. Overall, use *Imagexercise©* to become much more visually-oriented. This is a basic to improved performance.

8. In addition, use *Imagexercise©* to become a more systematic, organized and committed golfer and enjoy playing "within your game" and take pride in your golf scores.

How to Use Log Books and Journals for Imagexercising

Illustration 1

The Log Book illustrated at left is the most effective way of improving your application of imagery. The log book sketches each golf hole and should include the best landing areas for the hole and indications of slopes and contours around each green. The log book can have eighteen holes for each golf course you play regularly. Initially, use the log book for two purposes. First, do a series of *Imagexercise©* in which you visually hit each tee shot, each second shot, and the key shots around and on the green. Visualize before going to the golf course and again on each tee box. Second, make xerox copies of your log sheets and plot in each shot you hit. Do this after the game and then add your comments to your "Journal" (as illustrated, you can write technique and tenacity-type comments, etc. directly on your log book sheets).

Analysis - Illustration 1

The log shows slopes and traps. Second shot was imagexercised correctly but hit too far left and "up" on slope. In the journal comment, the golfer mentions positive grip technique and *Imagexercise©* performance.

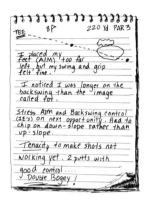

Illustration 2

Analysis - Illustration 2

In the entry the golfer noted incorrect foot placement on the drive. *Aim Line Imagexercise©* needed next shot. On technique, the grip was "comfortable" but backswing was too long and did not match the *Imagexercise©* of the swing needed. Drive was just left of ideal landing area and as a result of the second shot rolled beyond the idea area. There was a *Tactics Imagexercise©* problem and swing technique was the underlying reason.

Analysis - Illustration 3

Lots of chance of tactics error on this long hillside hole, but when drives hit the "flat" the extra roll leaves a 5 iron for this golfer. Here the golfer used two very demanding *Tactics Imagexercise©* and accomplished excellent results with shots to the "flat" and the only possible second shot landing spot, just in front of the green (left). Controlled putting on slight downhill green via *Tenacity Imagexercise©* on the green saved a nice two putt Par 4!

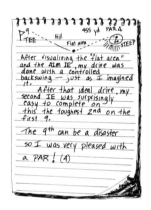

Illustration 3

These three illustrations are of log book and journal entries. The mapping stresses "local knowledge" and *Tactics Imagexercise©* that are necessary to improve this aspect of golf. Illustration 3 shows all three forms of *Imagexercise©* in making par on a demanding par 4 golf hole, a hole for which poor imagery skills could easily lead to a disastrous 6 or 7 or worse. Illustration 3 also stresses the demands of *Tenacity Imagexercise©* which allows the golfer to discipline and control putting and feel satisfaction as a result of mind control and golf performance.

Log books can be a key to improvement

Permanent Use of
Imagexercise©

There are some ways to increase the possibility of using *Imagexercise©* as a permanent part of your golf performance. The necessity for concentrating on "permanence" is due to the fact that imagery usage seems to vary from game to game. There are also many pre-game chances for usage and you will have to rehearse your swing and review your tactics. My experience was that I had to remind myself to use my imagery. Literally reemphasize imagery from time to time as necessary. It is easy to become imagery lazy!

Re-stressing your imagery

To Stress Imagery, Do The Following:

1. Use the log book, journal approach for at least one game per week.

2. Swing a golf club daily at home. Use a mirror or reflections from some large windows for matching your swing more closely to your set of precision *Technique Imagexercise©*.

3. Encourage yourself in using *Tenacity Imagexercise©*. Be tenacious on each green, on your pre-shot routine and in sandtraps or difficult recovery shots. You will find that you cut your score down and become consistent.

4. Work on pure ability to hold an image, to vary images and to make images vivid. Go back to review the quality of images and also do the imagery exercises in Chapter 4 of this book.

Getting Started in *Imagexercise©*

Evaluating yourself and your golf psyche:

1. Self Image

- First, have a clear purpose and a realistic goal for golf scores you expect. For several reasons your golf scores may not match up to your self-image in the rest of your life.

- Limit your psychologizing. It may be dangerous to overapply the mental end of golf. A few mental concepts well applied are vastly preferable to applying every mental idea to your golf psyche.

Evaluating yourself and your golf psyche

- *Accept a basic fact.* You may not play your best if you have had an unsettling day at the office or if your job or marriage is unsettled. This is normal. There are lots of days when it may be better not to play at all. If you recognize such days you will likely play much better when those circumstances are settled.

- In golf you can only be beaten by yourself. Very few are blessed with God-given golf skills. Play the course through *Imagexercise©* and soon everything will start to fall into place, and your opponents, your viewing public (i.e., your friends) and your golf will be under control.

- A certain level of arousal and aggression on the golf course is necessary. Channel your agression to your shotmaking and into completing your play for the game. If you had no plan or feel via imagery for a shot, do not kid yourself. Try to be prepared next time. *Use Your Intuition.*

- Do not try to "murder" a drive since it leads only to loss of body control and balance. Instead, put your rage into the best image swing you are capable of. This is a fine way to "settle up with the golf course."

- Every shot in golf is as important as every other shot - forget the missed ones. Missed putts are matched up by made putts. Do not lose your concentration.

- A missed shot in golf is not a disaster. Step back and relax. Shot #3 and shot #4 on any par 4 can make up for any disaster on prior shots.

- Use game management procedures since they are *Anti-Psych Out* in golf.

- Lots of things in golf are *not psychological.* Often golf is impaired by *fatigue, lack of course knowledge, bad weather or bad luck.*

Golf is not all psychological

Some Famous Self-Image Types Found on the Golf Course

Since the non-stop talker does not know the least about the mental side of golf or *Imagexercise©*, they try to use pure golf on the golf course with its many failings. Of course, pure golf requires near perfection and the nonstop talker is covering up for lack of perfection. They have no choice but to talk up a constant conversation of irrelevancies. In partner-golf play they apologize profusely, talk about new equipment, new balls and the latest gossip, or their latest golf lesson. Psychologically, the nonstop talker relieves feelings of ineptness and anxiety by constant talk to compensate for poor play. It is said that at least they are friendly if not dependable partners.

The clown is another "character," found in golf — although most often present in activity games such as tennis. Often the golf clown gives the impression that nothing matters as he or she quickly retees after a bad drive and hits another one (usually down the middle to reinforce his or her jovial giggling attitude). Often after a missed putt, he or she will bang the ball around the hole a few extra times to balloon their score to a 10 or a 12. Often they try to convince their foursome that nothing really matters, and today is the worst game they have ever played. Psychologically the golf clown is covering for temporary or permanent skill shortcomings.

Cobb, Kahn and Cath sketched these characters for Tennis (Psychology Today, June 1977). Here we have sketched a golf counterpart. The mental characters of sport are well described in sport and coaching literature (see bibliography).

The non-stop talker

The golf clown

Illustration by Jodi Lucas

Improving Your Golf Psyche with *Imagexercise©*

Guidelines

1. The application of *Imagexercise©* procedures to your own golf game will make it much easier for you to accept the difference between your actual self and the ideal self you envision in golf. This is due to a more realistic and feasible actual self and a modified vision of your ideal self.

2. *Imagexercise©* can only enhance golf performance for shots that you have seen performed and have practiced. The ideal self you envision in golf cannot include such special shots as Tom Watson's deep grass cut-lob shot* which made him famous. Unless you have seen that shot, understand the shape of the swing and clubface angle required, and have actually experienced that shot, you cannot program for that shot on the golf course. Your actual self-image and the ideal self you envision in golf will be much closer to one another as a result of this ability.

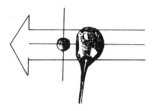

Know and practice the shots to be imaged

3. Psychologists tell us that if you have pride in yourself and self-worth off the golf course, you will likely be able to endure a badly played game on the golf course.

4. Inner dialogues or negative self-talk often lead to berating oneself for missing such "easy" shots in golf. Humiliation and cheating** are all too common in golf as a result of such harsh inner dialogue. In the principles of

---

* U.S. Open, 1982.

** The reader may object, but unfortunately it is true that cheating is all too common in golf. Humiliation may also be common. The author was, himself, witness to three cheating incidents in the last golf season - two in his amateur tournaments and one in a junior golf program. Surreptitiously dropping a replacement

Inner dialogues and negative self-talk

Imagexercise© we find it unnecessary to use self-destroying dialogue, instead keying in on the image and feel of the shot called for in our analysis of each shot situation. Failure to complete shots as planned and imaged will occur, but less frequently.

5. One's vision of oneself and one's golf play is normally a misleading illusion where mastery and control is overrated. By picking your level of entry in the hierarchical levels of learning in *Imagexercise©*, you will soon dissipate misleading illusions in favor of realistic shots, strategies and mental toughness more in keeping with your personality and your golf development.

6. Occurrences of assaults on a golfer's self-esteem are commonplace on the golf course. Well-meaning advice is the main culprit. Advice, although not allowed in the rules of golf, is nevertheless freely given when, in fact, 95 percent of the time the golfer does not need such advice. How often do you see husbands-wives, father-sons, and business associates "assisting" each other on the golf course?

No assaults allowed on a golfers self esteem

Insecurity created in this way hurts a golf game. If you sense or imagine a playing partner being overly critical of your game, it will destroy playing equilibrium. Often we play better towards the end of the game when we start to be more accepting of our playing partners. When your opponent apologizes for poor play after a few holes where your very best play just managed to beat him you may not continue to play well. If your self-esteem is strong off the golf course and if you have a good game plan and *Imagexercise©* program worked out, you will

ball, modifying a signed score card in a qualifying round and juniors in a threesome all turning in lowered scores are types of illegal practices. Interestingly, the codes of amateur golf were upheld by other golfers in the groups who checked the offender by reporting the infractions and in one case by sending the "cheater" off the golf course.

be strong in this aspect of maintaining your self-esteem. Psychological interventions for this situation will be found elsewhere in this book.

7. In golf we often play 'corners' or six holes with each of the foursome as a partner (or one-third of the game). If you believe you are turning the game into a nightmare for each of your partners, it is a harsh blow to your self esteem. Increased self consciousness leads to loss of self control and balance and further deteriorates your play in golf. Attempt to be less critical of yourself and devise a realistic plan for your contribution to the game. **Less self demand frequently provides better golf.**

Playing corners in golf

8. More literature and advice on the mental side of golf is available. One of the strongest bits of mental advice is regarding golfers learning to play the golf course and not their opponents (or their own psychological weaknesses). In essence, this is a wonderful opportunity to enhance self esteem and control self image by matching your golf game to the demands of the physical nature of the golf course. *Tactics Imagexercise©* and game management procedures open up easy ways to challenge and compete for each golfer while enhancing the social comraderie of even your staunchest opponent in golf. A friend of mine, an 8 handicapper from Canada, recently played a top Scottish amateur (one handicapper) in a Match Play Tournament at the Tassie Cup, a famous amateur tournament in Scotland. The Tournament at Carnoustie is played over the Links that are famous for fearsome hidden burns and narrow fairways such as 'Hogan's Alley', a hole made famous by Ben Hogan when he won The British Open. The Tassie matches are played off scratch so that no handicap allowances are given to either opponent. My friend was obviously in with a tough opponent and possibly in 'over his head' competition-wise. The only real hope was to play the course and not the opponent, for the eight handicapper. He would have to play *Tactics*

Play the course: Not your opponent

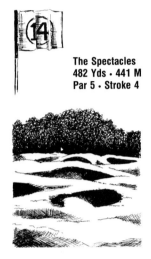

The Spectacles
482 Yds · 441 M
Par 5 · Stroke 4

Carnoustie Links

Imagexercise© only. Carnoustie has been rated as one of the toughest 'links' courses in the world. Founded in 1842, Carnoustie, Angus is according to the Encyclopedia of Golf "a long and exceedingly tough and challenging links". It was stretched to 7,252 yards for the 1968 British Open, when Gary Player won with 289. Hogan won there in 1953 (282). Henry Cotton in 1938 (290) and Tommy Armour in 1931 (296). Tom Watson won his first British Open in 1975 at Carnoustie.

My amateur friend managed to do as he had planned to do, keeping nearly level with his opponent. He won the 14th, a well planned birdie to be just one down, and halved the 15th and the 238 yard, par 3, 16th.

He kept referring to his *Imagexercise©* tactics maps and kept his mind off his opponent. Coming down the burn loops (i.e. winding creek) of 17, his opponent hit into the water of the famous Barry Burn driving too far and too much left. In the meantime, on 17, my friend hit an accurate drive. He followed by hitting his second in the big pot bunker guarding the left front of the green. With the penalty incurred his opponent hit a nervous but playable third, just off the green. Upon arriving at the pot bunker, my friend got a bit of the jolt when his ball lay too close to the front of the pot to go directly to the flag. His only choice was to blast out sideways. He did so. Now the ball lay 3 and the golden chance was seemingly slipping away.

His opponent chipped beautifully to within one foot and made 5. My friend's chip rolled 10' strong and his putt lipped and missed. So the match went to the one handicapper from Scotland.

There is a lot to be learned from matches such as the above. If an 'underdog' opponent has a strong game plan augmented with notes and imagery, he can sometimes do some unexpected winning, especially if the opponent plays 'pure golf'. After the match described

Lose without humiliation

above, the winner, upon shaking his opponent's hand, remarked how relieved he was to win the match and how unsettling it is to play an opponent who plays versus the course. Throughout the match he noticed his opponents tactics in playing the course.

Losing a match can be done without humiliation of loss of self esteem and a personal self image of success can remain intact. Psychologists agree that strong self esteem off the course is related to on the course esteem. Your self image and your golf game are inextricably linked to one another and as is often said, 'golf and games are life in miniature the majority of the time'.

Self-image and golf game are inextricably linked

Improving Your Golf Psyche and Avoiding Nervousness

Signs and Symptoms of Golf Nervousness Over a Shot

a) Your creative subconscious willingly accepts body messages sent to it so often you visualize 'disasters' instead of shot plans and positive images.

b) Muscle tension builds up.

c) You may breathe rapidly, even gasp.

d) Your feel or awareness of what the golf club (and your body) is doing is impaired.

Signs and symptoms

e) Your attention to shot analysis will suffer.

f) You may grab the first club that 'comes out at you' and miss hit a shot since you are using the wrong club.

Appropriate and Immediate* Imagexercise© Plan for Nervousness

a) Avoid the 'deadly trap', that is, do not strike the shot before you make a plan. The quick shot almost never works. (It seems that 95% of golfers in this situation react quickly, making the shot in an attempt to 'get it over with'! Perhaps it is true that they have little in the way of plans for such a shot).

Learn "your" shots and learn the image connected with hitting such shots

b) Devise a simple prompt *Imagexercise©* plan.

c) Analyze the situation for the best shot you are capable of striking, or coming close to striking that provides the least damage to an 18 hole golf score.

d) See an Imagexercise© minds eye picture of your relaxed calm approach to this or any such situation. This initiates control over (a) and (c) above.

e) Cement your relaxed, calm approach by seeing another *Imagexercise©* picture of other successful shots you have accomplished in similar 'nervous' situations. If you don't have the experience of having had such shots, you must learn what 'yours' are and learn the image connected with hitting such shots.

Rehearse these shots:

f) See an *Imagexercise©* picture of where you want the ball to logically finish up at.

g) See an *Imagexercise©* of the called for ball flight.

h) Finally see the swing and body action that you know will best result in the shot (Technique *Imagexercise©*).

i) During all of the above time, you are practice swinging or partial swinging or even "holding" the key part of the swing required to hit the shot. You are deeply into muscle memory. In this way, your subconscious will receive the key Technique *Imagexercise©*.

Muscle memory

Some golfers call this *muscle memory* or rehearsing with recapturing muscle feelings from previously similar shots that were successful.

j) Step and purposedly hit the shot.

* Lest you think this is a slow operation, it is not. By moving over to your shot location as promptly as possible, you will have the whole mini operation ready to go before it is your turn to hit.

Additional Points About (a) Through (k)

Please note: *Be very proud of your own ability* to cope or intervene and pull off an effective shot in golf. This is the most difficult thing to do successfully in *Sport*. Being humans, and not machines it cannot work every time or every shot, even for a PGA professional Tour player or other fine athlete. It will be successful if you are thorough! Again, store this whole occurrence in your head in your *Imagexercise©* file for the next time it is needed.

Only you know your past successes, so utilize them

Your Creative Sub-Conscious Thrives on such Occurrences So Use It!

This operation epitomizes the good feeling a golfer gets by being fully in charge. The 'high' feeling is augmented by *Imagexercise©* or other mental strategies. It matters little that the shot wasn't a classic one or a pro-like one. *It matters only that you got the best out of yourself* in that situation or challenge. You know you are capable at your own present level in this sport! *You are a performer!*

Your "high" comes from being fully in charge

Unless you are a successful Tour pro you won't win a wheelbarrow of $$$ — your 'high' is by being fully in charge — and it is a very good feeling indeed!

Some golfers do not feel it is worth the effort and 'trouble' to carry out such mental preparation and by way of example point to some golfers that are overly concerned with this part of the game. There is a happy medium of course. I can only say that such golfers will miss some sure satisfaction available in the game if they take the approach that mental golf isn't worthwhile.

This applies especially to the young successful (prodigy) golfer, who is superior in skill until he/she reach state or provincial level or National championship and then and only then need 'mental golf' to succeed. This thought applies as well on the Pro Tour where apparently survival is more critical and, as John Harris, the young All America golfer and Pro Tour dropout from Minnesota commented:

"The thinkers who can control their minds, rise to the top. They can concentrate, and they know when and how to relax".

Relaxation skills are consistently a necessity

Harris had mentioned how such golfers were like "precision machines" so far as their skill and golf games were concerned and that two other skills were found among the successful ones, namely *mental skills and relaxation skills!*

Common Irrational Beliefs and Golf

It is a catastrophy when things are not the way we like idea.

"I do my thing in golf" or "I am pleased with the demands I make of my golf game!"

Being pleased with your self-demands

Ask yourself "How often do I ask something unreasonable of myself?"

Imagexercise©
golfer

Common irrational belief occurence.

Positive imagactor

Unreasonable demand

Unreasonable image

Imagactor Golfer

Adapted from Ellis: Irrational Beliefs (Likely to Generate Anxiety). Ellis, A., Greiger, R. '77 Handbook of Rational Emotive Therapy, N.Y. Springer

Other Irrational Beliefs Likely to Create Golf Anxiety

1. **Worthwhile**, i.e. one must be thoroughly competent, adequate, and achieving in every way in order to be worthwhile.

2. **Approval**, i.e. it is necessary to be loved or approved of by virtually every other significant person.

3. **Happiness**, i.e. unhappiness and anxiety are externally caused and we have no control over our feelings.

4. **Threats**, i.e. if something is threatening or dangerous, one must keep thinking it might happen (closely related to Murphy's Law that if anything can go wrong, it will).

Source: *Ellis and Greiger, see above.*

Imagexercise© or being a positive 'imag-actor' can provide positive images for you, the golfer. Even for anxiety-provokers such as irrational beliefs or if things are not the way we would like. A golfer's self image is greatly enhanced through personal thoroughness in *Imagexercise©*.

Some golfers apparently suffer anxiety from their swing itself. John Updike, the accomplished author, **The Duffers Law** has described in Golf Digest Magazine how he is afraid of letting go of the earth (in golf) with the right foot during the golf swing and as a consequence he looks up, lifing his head the fatal "microsecond too soon" and thus ruins his swing. Updike is so sure this applies to many golfers that he has named this notion the *Duffer's Law.* If you don't get off the right side in your golf swing, everything goes wrong. The cure is of course, seeing a strong and vivid mental image of weight transfer and timing so that your body naturally listens to your image-selector in your right brain, prior to each golf swing. As a consequence anxiety is not possible with a positive imagery procedure, just as it is not with irrational beliefs and golf, *unless you let it!*

Relaxation, Enjoyment, Fitness and *Imagexercise©*

Preparing to use *Imagexercise©* will be enhanced by an ability to relax while playing golf. A feeling of enjoyment of the niceties of golf is also not only enhancing to the mental efforts in golf but enjoyment of the game is more likely to occur through mental golf. Some golfers consider that it is totally enjoyable to practice and play the game, and if you don't, you should take up other recreational pursuits, at least temporarily. During golf season take off a few days from golf completely. When my off season sport of ice hockey in the Oldtimers League becomes a bore or drag, one good reaction is to take a week or two off. The same applies to persisting injury. In hockey, we have 21 players and need only twelve skaters per game. Our game philosophy for hockey expects players to miss due to mental factors, injury, family and job committments. In the same way, golf is there for life enhancement, so use golf in that manner.

The Best of all Games

Ben Hogan is known to have held the view that golf was interesting, demanding and rewarding and the best of all games. Even when heading to the practice tee, he said he felt privileged and happy for he couldn't wait for the sun to come up the next morning, so he could get out on the course again.

Hogan's notions on enjoying golf are not universally held. For example, Lee Trevino believes that golf is nerve wracking enough, so he desperately tries to keep his old at home routines where possible. Trevino disdains fast cars, for example, while many Tour pros drive fast cars and drive them fast. In a recent golf exhibition in Calgary, Canada, Trevino felt both he and his wife needed security guards. While Calgary is a big, bustling city, it hardly is known to require security at the worst of times.

Lee Trevino

Golfers probably should be familiar with relaxation techniques such as Jacobsen's or other popular positive mind control relaxation done on the progressive principles. Any good sports psychology book will provide such a program for you, the reader.

Earlier we had noted the fact that fitness conscious people are among those that utilize imagery well in their life. The reader is referred to recent golf articles about now famous PGA Ladies Tour golfer, Patty Sheehan. Sheehan has a tremendously well thought out lifestyle, and her ability to budget her time for a well rounded daily schedule, including fitness, is basic to her consistency in life and in golf. Patty Sheehan is a role model, to be sure, and in 1984 she became the first LPGA player to win a huge bonus award of a half million dollars for winning consecutive golf tournaments.

Budget time for fitness and golf preparation

Patty Sheehan outlined her views on consistency and life style even more in 1985. Besides winning the bonus during 1984 for winning two consecutive times, Sheehan inadvertently prevented Alice Miller, the new Tour sensation and leading money winner from winning the new bonus of $1 million, when she nudged Miller by 2 strokes in the bonus tournament.

Weight Training and Flexibility Exercises for Golf

It is often viewed that well toned muscles and flexible muscles will aid the golf swing *but it is certainly true that imagery can be applied with greater confidence* in such a golfer.

The author works on light weight training and flexibility for golf three times a week and his program will be found in the appendix.

Becoming a Successful Golfer

The main factors for novice, intermediate, advanced, Club pro and Tour pro of the 1980s and 1990s.

Stages for Becoming a Successful Golfer

Novice to Advanced Beginner	Gaining skill, gaining experience, little golf fitness, some use of mental golf	Some benefit of Imagexercise

Goals of a non-full-time golfer

Intermediate to near Advanced	Less time on skill practice, gaining experience, initial use of regular mental golf, better golf fitness and plays regularly	Considerable benefit from Imagexercise possible

Advanced or top club golfer	Top use of mental golf, plays lots, a golf fit person	Regular use and regular benefit of Imagexercise type program

Full-time amateur, some club professionals, PGA Tour players	Skill maintenance, keeps golf fit, tends to be a successful psychological golfer	Tends to be successful psychological golfer

The new sports wave in golf consists of Tour players, swing instructors and mental enhancers working together.

Strictly limited in numbers, survival level only. Risky.	Experience re-cycler, practices lots	

Pure Physical Practice and Intuition

Pure Physical Practice (PPP), and Intuition give improved golf shots.

Main Loop and Recycle Loops of Golf Improvement

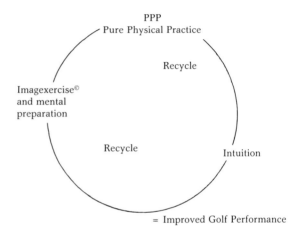

Main Loop

PPP
Pure Physical Practice

Recycle

Imagexercise©
and mental
preparation

Recycle

Intuition

Intuition has to be repected and utilized

= Improved Golf Performance

Intuition should be respected and utilized in combination with *Imagexercise©* for a golf shot, along with pregame pure physical practice and brief pre-shot physical practice.

Improved Golf Shots

Notes for Main Loops and Recycle Loops of Golf Improvement

Common areas of intuitive thinking in golf may often include how to play a shot in the wind; how shot requirements change from a morning to an afternoon round; cueing in on 'better knowledge' of a golf hole, as if in a 'gestalt' (i.e. in a 'whole thought' type moment you really see how a hole 'should' be played); picking up a cue from another golfer; and/or hitting stronger shots as you get "pumped up" from the effect of playing better,

The H Adrenaline golf reaction

and your adjustments to being "pumped up". (H Adrenaline type reaction).

Recollection of a former, similar experience as you play a similar hole or situation *or* keying in on a recorded post-game analysis from prior games are also sources of side-loop intuition.

PPP or Pure Physical Practice still has a very large role in golf improvement when practice is correct and precise. Primary ways to gain the most in PPP, besides using accurate imagery as you practice, are feedback or knowledge of results and pure ball striking (repetitive) practice itself. For example, take "Selective Practice" which I describe as follows. Select out three balls and your 150 yard iron (4, 5, 6 or 7 iron). Land ball #1 left of a 150 yard marker, land ball #2 over top of the marker and land ball #3 just to the right of the marker. Repeat this three ball cycle. Check your alignment (and use a T-line *Imagexercise©*) Constantly change aim but utilize swing similarity and controlled striking. You can precede selective practice three ball striking with PPP (Repetitive hitting after a shoulder flexibility warm-up) and use KR (Knowledge of Results, i.e. where ball is landing and how it is flying) to adjust your pure practice.

PPP: The role of Pure Physical Practice

Knowledge of results

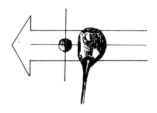

PPP also involves several other aspects that although ranked as relatively insignificant for golf learning, may be very important to certain golfers. You may find them not only intriguing and useful but also things you have wondered about as you have practiced in the past. They have been named by motor learning sport scientists as Massed vs Distributed practice (i.e., when do you rest?); scheduling of practice (another fatigue factor); variability in practice (should practice vary like a game varies?); individual difference in practice (females thrive on variability in practice!); motivation (authenticity of your reasons for practice); behavior modification (i.e. how much 'scheduled approval' do you thrive on?); social motivator (i.e., only practicing on the putting green for social and challenge reasons (putt for nickels, for dollars or impressing someone) *or* only hit balls when you can show-off your swing and/or talk; transfer effects (the practice

Social motivation to practice for some golfers

and trap was so much easier than those on the golf course, that despite practicing, there was no transfer effect).

CHAPTER THREE
SUMMARY OF THE CHAPTER

Key words and notions of this chapter.

- Some basic *Imagexercises*© to be found in Chapter 3 are: Aimline IE, Shotshape IE, Ball landing behaviour IE, Swing rhythm IE, Swing shape IE, Clubface position and wrist pronation IE, and capturing good swing feel IE.

- Communicating with your subconscious about patience and your ability to get organized is illustrated.

- Knowing golf assets and liabilities of your swing and game is detailed as is tempo recapturing.

- Knowing how far your game can take you is a golf ability.

- Eight basic ways of using *Imagexercise*© are outlined.

- Using log books and journals is illustrated by reference to actual golf situations.

- Excellent ways to make imagery a better, more permanent skill are outlined.

- Ways to evaluate your golf psyche and self image for golf are included.

- The notion that less self-demand gives better golf is explained.

- A great *Tactics Imagexercise*© is covered - the illustration of learning to play the course and not the opponent.

- The most difficult thing to do in sport is something you can do.

- Golf is a chance to marshall fitness, relaxation and enjoyment.

- *Intuition* as well as pure physical golf practice (PPP) are the other means to improved shots and their basics are mentioned.

Chapter 4
Improving Your Image Making Ability

Objectives:

This chapter includes a set of progressive visualiza-tion exercises; golf examples for all exercises, some basic general exercises; relaxation practice; a viewing room and screen notion; notes on training time; advice from Psychology in India (Yogic/Tantric); restressing principles; customizing your imagery pro-gram, self tests, tracking; visual skills and reminders, conviction notes, ideas on tapering off and transfer to golf games; building a skill basis; and the full time mental-usage golfer.

Definition of Imagexercise©

The whole text of our book has been built around the two aspects of imagery and golf:

1. An image itself.
2. Practice with that image. Either the image alone or in combination with the sport of golf. Often the image is found in golf practice.

This chapter will assist the reader with:

1. Techniques of producing and controlling images so that they have a positive and demonstrated effectiveness in golf.
2. Techniques for practicing or playing while using these images in a positive, often effec-tive, sports performance.

Imagexercise© is Susceptible to Improvement

As Connolly and Syer stated in their book *Sporting Body, Sporting Mind*, consciously or unconsciously we are all adept at visual thinking. We all use images in everyday life. However, our images in a specific game such as golf may not be readily available to our brain. You may feel your golf images are fuzzy or inaccurate. This chapter is solely devoted to the improvement of your image-making ability. Schools and other institutions may have inadvertently truncated some of our natural visual thinking ability. Rediscovery or improvement of visualization or imagery is possible for most people. The step from visual thinking to visualization (and "imagexercising") is similar to the step from natural sporting ability to sophisticated technical and tactical skill. The skill of generating images for golf and using the images for tactics, stroke improvement and consistency and for mental tenacity can be learned just as can your physical performance skills. It is to be kept in mind that, as in any physical skill, the ability to create and apply powerful sports imagery needs to be taught and practiced regularly should you expect consistent and noticeable improvement in your performance.

Practice with your image

It is usually true that using mental skills to augment your golf performance requires some practice and development. With time the golfer-athlete can expect to become proficient in using image skills. Eventually this way of combining mental and physical golf can become as second nature to you as heading out to the golf course itself. Golfers have reported lower golf scores by simply reading about visualizing in golf, but to organize and practice imagery golf can provide sure score reduction.

Eventually, combining mental and physical golf can become second nature to you

What this chapter proposes to do, is to take you from infrequent use of Visualization in golf to frequent and effective use. You will sell yourself on Imagexercise© *as soon as the following happens to you:*

At the most unexpected time you will sink a long putt. The long putt will go in because you visually track the ball up to and into the hole several times. The putt might be so long that you would be happy just to get it near the hole. However, you will find

that the fact you visualized carefully will surprise you because you will make the putt. Already this golf season I have sunk a seventy yard wedge shot and a ninety yard shot. The ninety yard shot went directly into the hole for an eagle three. It appears that the reason these shots went in was because I imagexercised the ball flight and the bounce and roll right into the cup. I remember distinctly that I was worried on the ninety yarder that I might not even hit the green because the shot was from behind a small tree. So I told myself to slow down in preparing for the shot and imagine the ball going into the hole at least three times. The ball did exactly as I had imagined!!

Practice will make you comfortable with visualizing

Some weeks after writing this chapter, I was playing a golf game with a foursome in a Level II golf class and I remembered to imagexercise thoroughly on a 150 yard third shot on a long par 5 hole. The ball hit the green and disappeared. When we arrived on the contoured green, the ball was found in the cup and not past the green as we expected. This chapter will provide exercises to practice pure visualizing. Practice will make you comfortable with visualizing. Hopefully you will become sure of yourself with your golf imagery. Practice will make it easier to recall vivid and golf-accurate mind's eye pictures from your subconscious.

When Are Your Images Really Images?

Remember that you already know how to visualize. In driving your car, in anticipating good food and in your body self concept, you rely on mind pictures. When you go to a golf driving range you may see some amazing contortions "parading" as golf swings. Look again and select only those swings that have some good mechanics of efficient golf motions. Notice that already you are capable of this type of imagery. Close your eyes and run a set of swing pictures through your mind. Include some of the golf motions you saw at the driving range. Very impressive, isn't it?? Just think! Here you have a portable set of swing pictures that will do much more for your golf game and score than a good set of golf clubs will ever do! All you need is a larger set of accurate golf images and your score will literally drop out of sight!! Perhaps all you require is better visual skills.

Pure Visualization Exercises

Let us set out the key area to concentrate upon in our sport visualization exercises. *Use a Simple Guideline.* Better concentration, better relaxation and sport vision produces better images in golf. You must be motivated but relaxed and in a state of what is called "easy" concentration. Forcing visualization tends to extinguish it just as the visual starts to appear, which is why you should practice the following exercises for short, relaxed periods of time. Visualization is very individual and your colors may vary with the "original" scene you are imitating in your mind's eye. When people first begin to visualize, the images they see are often different from the images you "get" from the retina of your eye. These "different" images can still be sport-effective however.

It is quite often found that the imager almost feels that he is "making up" mind pictures. Mental images often have more resemblance to thoughts and ideas than to sights. After practicing for several days you will begin to be pleased with the development of the actual "sight" images that you generate. These images will become more like the golf accurate scenes you require. Almost all my images on putting greens are done with my eyes open (with my two hands shading my eyes) but you should practice these exercises with your eyes closed. I believe that eyes closed imagery is the more effective form of using images in golf. Personally, however, I sometimes have my eyes open and try to imagine the ball rotating to the hole. Also my eyes are open for ball tracking and ball bounce and roll imaging. Practice these exercises with eyes closed and you will later find that brief eyes closed golf scenes come to you more readily on the golf course.

Brief eyes-closed golf scenes come to you more readily on the golf course

Exercise 1: Concentrated Breathing.

One effective way to get ready for visualization practice is to count breaths for sixty seconds or longer. Visualize yourself sitting back in a soft chair, relaxing your body until it produces tension-free tingling while you start noticing your inhale, exhale cycle. Count these cycles. Concentrate only on your breathing and when extraneous thoughts enter into your mind, let them pass through. Expect distractions but simply shuttle them on through without any effect at all. Return to counting breaths. Slowly improve your concentrated breathing ability. If you lose track of your count, try again. Use the *Zen* metaphor for intruding thoughts - thoughts are like birds flying across the sky of your mind. They will pass through - let them. This is a handy skill on the golf course. Notice that you are better off if you concentrate on one image. Notice too, that you are capable what of the Yogas and Sufis call heightened awareness. Return to this exercise each day you practice. You can easily combine an image of a lung inflating and deflating as you count. The key, however, is to learn to concentrate and to be in control. Later this skill will be used to narrow down to the one key golf image you require.

You are better off if you concentrate on one key image

Exercise 2: Visualizing a Triangle.

Place this triangle illustration in line with your eyes. Sit in your soft chair and feel your body progressively relax. Take the time to feel the difference between tense and relaxed muscles. Breath smoothly and deeply. Look at all aspects of the triangle and see the gradations of grey in the background. Close your eyes and bring the triangle to your mind's eye. See as much detail of color and shape as you can. The geometric shape produces a visualization of grey and black background and white contrast. Some people see shades of reds (I tend to see reds and shades of red) for the triangle or some other color contrast in the mind's eye. The triangle visualization produces vivid or sharper imagery and also illustrates that we must accept various levels of visual ability.

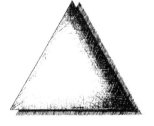

If a person is Negative about his ability to visualize the triangle he can extinguish the image and not get the practice benefit!!

Exercise 3: Visualizing a Small Object.

Use a light bulb, a shiny apple, or a glossy golf tee for this exercise. Take in the whole object, let's say the golf tee, as you view it. Look directly at it. Eyes open. Think only of the object. Notice its size, its shine, its shape, its smoothness, its color, its grain and its varying roundness. If intruding thoughts come to you, let them pass and go back to concentrating. How well can you concentrate? Is a minute a standard you can attain? Your mind may want to wander but don't let it. This ability to concentrate and then use an image of the object will be the same as your improved golf course ability to concentrate on and image an exact landing spot on a golf shot.

After viewing the object, close your eyes and see if you can bring the object before your mind's eye. Relax and don't try too hard. Be "soft" with your attempts to visualize and you will soon improve your visualization skill.

Exercise 4: Visualizing a Favorite Room.

Use visualization to visit a favorite room from your childhood or a favorite clubhouse. See the details that you remember the best. See favorite chairs, the woodwork and the "comfort" of the room. See yourself relaxing in this room and visualizing the views that come easily to your mind. Psychologists feel that this is one of the easiest visualizations to recollect. Visualize some of the activities that you used to do in this favorite room.

If it is a golf clubhouse with good views of a golf course, visualize the best of the views.

Exercise 5: A Visualization of Moving
Around an Object.

Use your visualization to move around the outside of a favorite house or golf clubhouse. Walk around all sides and examine it closely. "Zoom" in for a close up of some details. See a full view of some of the features that interest you. See your favorite viewlines of the house or clubhouse as if you were looking at them from your most recollectible sightlines. Can you visualize some of the classic clubhouses in golf such as Pinehurst, Royal Troon or St.Andrews?

Exercise 6: See Around a Detailed Object and an Object that has Subtle Differences in It.

Stand a favorite golf bag up in a tripod golf stand and view it from all angles. Walk around it and move your visualization angles constantly. View it from above. See the sides and the front view. See a visualization of the bag lying on the green grass. Your consciousness that supplies images can move at your will. See that your mind is a slide projector with an infinite number of slides in its storage files. Without moving greatly you have seen a great variety of viewing angles.

Visualize the subtle differences of the 3 iron through the 9 iron in the graphic at right. Close your eyes and see the difference between the 3, 6 and 9 iron. You can almost see the ball leaving these clubfaces at three different angles. Observe your own irons for every detail of their character as well.

Visualize the differences of the 3, 6 and 9 iron

Exercise 7: Visualizing Golf Balls.

Imagine that you are seeing the three balls from above, below and from the side. Visualize the three labels noticing the styles of print and the various angles of the lettering. As a self test, can you recollect in your imagery the lettering styles of the Titleist, the Pro Staff and the Top Flite balls? Visualize three other balls such as the Ping, the Golden Ram and the Tracer.

Visualize the balls rolling towards you as you crouch behind the hole sighting in a putt. Do this with eyes closed and then with eyes open. Visualize the ball roll and the letters rotate as if they are moving without any wobble. See the letters fall into the exact middle of the golf hole. Visualize for each color in your mind's eye. Use a Ping two tone ball and you will be able to path a rolling putt with exacting effectiveness. Visualize that you are practicing a variety of chip shot angles with colored or optic golf balls. You will soon chip more effectively since you will have stored images for ball path and various angles of ball movement off golf clubs of various lofts.

Notice that you are now combining Imagination with Imagery.

Visualize the ball rolling into the cup

Try holding a labelled, colored golf ball and rotate it as if it were rolling towards the cup or hole on a green. Sight just over the top of the ball towards a real golf hole. Then set the ball down, lettering facing the exact middle of the hole and putt the ball into the cup. Practice all of your visualizations of ball rotations three times each so that you will remember to do the same on the golf course.

Exercise 8: Controlling Your Image.

Visualize yourself returning to a familiar golf locker room. As you enter, turn on the light and notice the familiar parts of the room. Turn the switch off and on, and recheck the details in your visualization. Go over to a window that overlooks a putting green. Use this opportunity to "float" out the window and view the contour of the green. Notice the putts that will be subjected to considerable contour roll. Gently "float" down to the green, putt on the holes that you had noticed. Notice that you are now exhibiting considerable control over your images. You control the light and the dark and the angles of view just as required in *Tactics Imagexercising©*.

Exercise 9: Visualize a Person.

Visualize another golfer with whom you can play a game. Notice his golf glove. Notice the shoes he chooses to wear. Notice his facial expression. Do you see a calm, impatient or harried look on his face?

Now visualize his movement as he does a basic skill such as teeing up a ball or taking a practice swing with his driver. This exercise teaches you to visualize another person who is moving or doing movements. Realize that your daydreams are infinitely rich visualizations. Use these daydreams for improving image control.

Exercise 10: Visualize Yourself and Your
Movements.

Imagine yourself from the time you are in a
locker room to the time you walk onto the practice
or 1st tee. Join some friends and see yourself hit
a few balls as you chat with them. Step outside of
"yourself" as you do an external image of one of
your golf swing movements. Imagine the feel you
get on those first few hits! See yourself as taking
it really easy as you build up to a nice tempo in
your swing. Zoom in for a close-up of your hand-
action and see and feel little hand tension. Hear a
click of center-to-center contact between ball and
club. Hear yourself explaining your good golf swing.

Do not be impressed by the good players practicing, rather see an image of your own practice system and your own thorough preparation. Do not
tire yourself out, instead get your golf mind
prepared.

Zoom in on a part of the golf swing

Exercise 11: Visualization of Your Favorite
Scene.

Close your eyes and relax your muscles as you
ease your mind's eye into one of your favorite visual
reveries.

Notice the fine details of your scene, the light
dancing on the water, the sunrise or sunset that
allows you to visualize with ease. Pick out a favorite action you might enjoy and imagine your own
details.

Notice how you tend to feel happy and sure of
yourself. Enjoy a fine moment for you and your
consciousness.

What would you be doing in your favorite scene?
What does your visualization have your sense of
hearing, feel, touch and smell doing?

Exercise 12: Body Response to your
Visualization Practice.

Imagine that one arm is holding a couple of books
or boxes of golf balls. The other is being "supported" by a balloon that floats above your arm.

As you close your eyes and visualize this exercise, you will feel your arms move slightly in

response to the imagined resistances. *Your body does respond to Visual Images.* ''Feel'' your golf clubs via the same exercise in your imagination.

Exercise 13: Visualization of a Special Image Viewing Room or Studio.

Visualization practice is often done in a private area or favorite room. Use this exercise to further develop this facility. Include a viewing screen so that you can preview your golf technique, the golf course you intend to play and the *Tenacity Imagexercise©* you will require for mentally productive golf.

As you visualize your viewing ''retreat'' make it as comfortable and as ''sports'' enhanced as you would if you could actually design and build such a facility. Note all the details of warmth and color. Add a clock so that you can complete imagery exercises for many programs of golf preparation.

Also notice in your mind's eye that you can devise new images for lowering your golf score while practicing in your image viewing room.

This viewing room is a facility or space that you can return to anytime you wish, no matter what you may be involved in at the moment. Return anytime that you wish, to work, to think, to imagine, or just to feel good. Artists and writers need such a space and so does a creative golfer. Plan your golf practice sessions by visualization in your viewing room.

Exercise 14: Using Confidence Rather than Doubt Exercise.

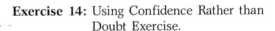

In this exercise you use a ''saying'' or strategy statement as a suggestion to your visualization brain. As in a prayer, you visualize and associate with confidence, not with doubt. Follow up this exercise with golf visualizations.

It is not true that visualization ''turns-on'' one day and ''turns off'' the next, although this will happen if you let it, if you don't use exercises such as Exercise 14.

When Joan Joyce, a former professional softball player became a LPGA Tour golfer in 1977, it was not long before this long hitter set a new record during the Michelob Tournament of just 17 putts in 18 holes. She said her secret that day was visualizing. She also said she visualized ball tracking and the ball dropping into the hole. If she had good images every day there would be no telling how well she could play the Tour. She said that images were not something she could turn on and off.

Visualize the ball tracking and dropping into the hole

Exercises 13 and 14 are designed to make visualization a daily occurrence. To further develop confidence in your visual imagery ability, see the books by Singer, Horowitz, McKim and Castenada listed in the Bibliography.

Exercise 15: Strategy Statement for Confident *Imagexercise©*.

Relax as you close your eyes and visually travel to the most comforting golf course or retreat you have ever visited. Tell yourself how "deeply" relaxed you are. Sit down and view the deep serenity of this peaceful area of green space and growth. Your mind is clear and satisfied, and your body is strong and supportive. See how receptive your mind is to your clear golf images and strengthen these images.

Exercise 16: Getting in Touch with Your Present Visualization.

To change or upgrade your present visualizations about golf (or other visualizations) it will be necessary to get in touch with your present ones. Return to your image viewing room or studio and start to assess some of your current images in golf. Look at those that appear to be uncertain. Then replan a series of changed images based on new, accurate and specific golf information for technique, tactics and tenacity. Review a few of these on your golf viewing screen until you are able to visualize them with confidence.

Go back to Exercise 15 as often as necessary. Keep in mind the information given to you in Chapter 1 where the reason images worked was explained. A detailed and specific image gives a specific effect. If you see your front arm as a long lever in the golf swing then an image of a long lever will help your body provide such a lever. Your central nervous system requires and uses specific impulses from images. This means you can recall a former performance and improve it. Remember the good ball striking you have had in the past. That is your link to more good ball striking.

Exercise 17: Repetitive Imagery Rehearsal.

It is extremely effective to exercise the same image sequence repeatedly in golf. For example, a full *Tactics* rehearsal of a golf course can be completed in a few minutes. Repeat this exercise six or eight times and your right brain and subconscious brain will be fully available to make certain you play the course in the best way you have visualized it.

The Key to Exercise 17 is repeatability in Imagexercising©.

Detailed and repeated visualization of skills and assets you may wish to acquire can be done. It is best to keep these wishes private and confidential but rest assured that you can, in fact, acquire them via visualization. Read about creative visualization in the book by Wiehl and Opthiel for further ideas.

Some Tips in Carrying Out Exercise for Improved Imagery

Improve your imagery in nine ways

- Easy concentration or easy imagining practice days are the days that you can image with added vividness. Ability to hold an image is directly affected by ease of concentration in imagining.

- Improvement in ability to hold clear golf images will be gradual.

- The colors of your imagery will gradually improve.

- Do not stress verbal reactions or start to label images in exercising for images; *instead* stress feelings and the experience that the object itself suggests.

- Learn to control intruding thoughts while practicing imagery by letting those thoughts pass by.

- Set some easily attainable goals (thirty second; sixty second; two minutes; five minutes; or occasionally longer sessions per exercise).
- Practice zooming in on an image as if you were a movie or video camera.
- See an object from various points of view. For example, in Exercise 3, see a low tee, see a high tee, see a row of tees or see a tee forming a V with another tee. See various golfers holding those tees. Break away from habitual ways of viewing things! Break away from habitual labels and see the added potential of the way in which you view things. This creates a self-view as if you were continuing to become a proficient user of visualization/imagery skills.
- Set a number of small objects on a green table cloth and see how many objects you can hold in your mind's eye imagery. Check the details by opening your eyes and then check the details of your images accuracy.

Some Key Tips On Relaxing Your Body

1. Learn the difference in the feeling of a muscle tightening and a muscle loosening or relaxing.

2. Practice by progressively putting a muscle under tension and slowly making that same muscle relax.

Modify your relaxation skills for the golf course

3. Go through all the major muscle groups and practice muscle relaxing one group or one body part at a time.

4. Start with large muscles and progress towards smaller muscles.

5. Use images that suggest to your subconscious a relaxed state or stretch.

6. Practice relaxing in a comfortable lying position (often lying on your side).

7. Practice relaxing while sitting with your legs stretched out in front of you.

8. Sit on a bench behind the tee boxes and do this form of relaxing.

9. Try to learn to relax your leg, shoulder, chest, back and arm muscles as you walk down a fairway.

Be Positive about relaxing and you will see Positive results.

Da Vinci Device for Imagery Enhancement

Professor R. McKim of Stanford University teaches a course in experiences in visual thinking. As a child, you probably did visual thinking as you lay on your back and watched fluffy clouds roll by. Those clouds suggest many shapes to the viewer. McKim says that daVinci thought that random imaginings stimulated imaginative seeing. In the daVinci device, you look at paint stains, wall cracks or old paint chips and then look for imaginative resemblances such as animal shapes, figures or even entire landscapes.

Professor McKim of Stanford

Motivation and Imagery

Motivation plays such a tremendous part in developing enhanced imagery that it is imperative that the golfer who sets out to improve his skill in imagery has a set of goal statements to take account of his present state of image attainment. Goals usually encourage committment.

Long term and short term goals

Setting Imagery Improvement Goals

It may be reasonable to attempt each of the seventeen basic imagery golf exercises for just one minute each or for one seventeen minute practice session.

Another reasonable goal might be success in one or two of the seventeen exercises. The next goal for the next week of practice might be three or four of the seventeen exercises. Success means image clarity and image holding ability. Set new goals as you proceed and as you achieve success.

During the golf season, it might be reasonable to set initial goals for six of the eighteen holes. It might also be a reasonable goal to stress putting green imagery at first. Later a golfer can add *Tactics* imagery for every golf hole. *Tenacity* images for difficult situations eventually will be worked into the golfer's overall image system.

Post-game image analysis is extremely self-motivating since a repeated image success is likely to become internalized. Small successes build larger successes and overall confidence.

Training Time for Mental Preparation and Practice

Pre-Season:
One to two hours every second day with focus upon
a) improving images;
b) working with PGA professional so that you increase your knowledge of the golf swing

In Season:
Pre-Game:
Thirty minutes. Focus on *Tactics Imagexercise©*
Game:
During pre-shot phases on the tees, approach shots and on the greens
Post Game:
Fifteen minutes. Two basic post game analyses as outlined in this chapter.

Post Season:
Summarize all your diary notes and write new objectives for golf and systematic imagery. Also do refresher reading for *Tactics* on new sport technology ideas. Weight train or do other sports in which imagery plays some role.

Developing Golf Realism

Accept the fact that all of your *Technique Imagexercise©* will not always deliver good shots. The idea is to deliver fewer poor shots and to come closer to delivering a greater percentage of good shots. As your imagery improves, you will come closer to golf realism. Tom Watson and other Tour Professionals stress the idea of playing each shot as if it was a completely new situation. *You should too!*

Complete Your *Imagexercise*© Bank

As you improve your ability to use imagery in golf, try to make your *Imagexercise*© *Bank* as complete as possible. For example, it is important that you recall or are capable or recalling to your mind's eye an image for each part of the golf swing. See a picture of what your hands and wrists are to do and see a clear picture of your footwork. Prevent vagueness on the golf course!

In other words your goal is to have an image bank you can trust. Trusting your images directly affects your golf confidence. You will have clarity, timing and completeness of images available to you on the golf course. Intimidation will not affect your golf. You will be able to turn your concentration on and off.

Penny Pulz

When Penny Pulz, a young Australian Tour professional had one of her best years, she had a positive attitude because she could turn on her concentration just as you will through your complete imagery bank. You will not have to expect golf miracles.

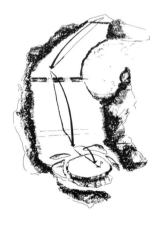

Overconcentration and Freewheeling It

As has been stressed in *Tactics Imagexercise*© it is important to preview the way that you are going to play a hole either before the game or while standing on the tee box. Do not prevent those shots from taking place by steering the ball around the course. Get completely out of left brain analysis and feel that good swing as you waggle or do your pre-hit preparation. Then swing away freely!

Allen Miller, a young Tour Pro, once became so disgusted with his shots on Tour that he had to remind himself to freewheel and not to worry or overconcentrate. He said his game would fall apart if he didn't freewheel it.

Common Pitfall in *Imagexercise©* Use

Inadvertent Imagexercise Replacement

Leads to: Golfer losing composure because external environment takes over. For example, the golfer starts to lose focus on specific *Imagexercise©* and instead focuses on or is too impressed by other golfer and loses his game plan.

Often gets too involved with Self!!

The practice of *Imagexercise©* is based on the golfer selecting correct images based on individual golf needs. Each golfer has technique and tactics needs, and specific areas of mental toughness need. The basic idea in *Imagexercise©* is to select a few images for each golf game. Know your needs or make an intelligent assessment of your needs and then stick with them. This results in mind control. This prevents inadvertent *Imagexercise©* replacement. Clear images, well adhered to prevent self-focus from ruining a good golf game. There is no need to be impressed by other golfers! *Each golfer needs his own plan.* If another golfer offers you advice, don't let that disrupt your image plan. Ask him to save his advice for a more appropriate time. He will understand!

Imagexercise© and Concentration Keys

1. Loss of concentration can be prevented by focusing on one or two imagery keys in a systematic, repetitive manner.

2. Select imagery by looking for tell-tale *Cues* from similar game situations and the golf course itself.

3. Pair cues with imagery that has worked in the past. Quality images will produce quality results.

4. Focusing attention based on your golf strengths and weaknesses will reduce anxiety and multiply your ability to concentrate.

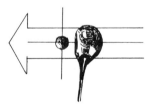

The eight concentration keys

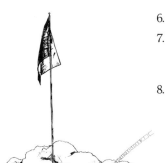

5. Have a game plan. Stick with your game plan for all eighteen holes. Start using your imagery plan from the first shot and set a tone for your concentration.

6. Use the same imagery that you have rehearsed.

7. Develop a narrow focus rather than a wide one and you will find that it will produce concentration in golf.

8. Enjoy moments in which you turn concentration off but remain convinced that your concentration can be turned back on when you require it. You do not need "tunnel concentration," what you need is the ability to turn it on and off, as Lee Trevino appears to be capable of doing.

Keep your Imagery in disguise as much as possible, remembering that Imagery is your private game plan.

Post Game Analysis for Checking Your Game Use of Imagery

Procedure: There are three steps that the golfer should use when checking for effectiveness of golf imagery. Do this procedure as soon as possible after playing. These steps are a step-by-step analysis that has been called a program of cognitive training in sport.

The *first step* is to focus on the key listed number 1. The *second step* is to ask yourself the basic self analysis question listed and the *third step* is to restate and re-image the preferred outcome (called the *Positive Imag Actor*). The preferred outcome, is of course, the shot or strategy that you would have ideally accomplished on the golf course.

Study and then practice the following examples after 18 holes of actual golf.

Example 1

Step 1: An Excellent Game Score and Feeling Associated (KEY)

(*also* use an excellent hole score)

Step 2: Basic Self Analysis Question.
"What did your stable quiet mind or
your calm icy feeling actually feel like
as you played golf today?"

Step 3: Rehearse a Positive *Imag Actor.*
i.e. My positive Imag Actor is a mind's
eye of my golf when shot selection
seemed to come off very well and
calmness was good. Repeat this Imag
Actor as an image several times.

**Three steps to use for
checking your golf imagery**

Example 2

Step 1: Poor Game and Associated Feeling.
(KEY)
Step 2: Basic Self Analysis Question.
"What did it feel like when I had a
hard time settling my feelings down
during an 18 hole game?"
Step 3: Rehearse a Positive *Imag Actor.*
e.g. My positive Imag Actor shows me
getting complete control of one or two
key feelings right away.

Example 3

Step 1: Specific Competitive Scenes
(KEY) and Arousal.
Step 2: Basic Self Analysis Question.
"Was it my trap shots or something
else that altered my physical reactions
or the normally successful way I carry
out my trap shot procedures?"
Step 3: Rehearse a Positive *Imag Actor.*
e.g. Carry out an imagery rehearsal of
your sand shot technique and shot
procedure (in this case, go for some
extra practice to reaffirm your shot
procedure in sand traps. Stress tough
shots and reinforce your tenacity).

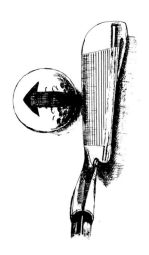

Example 4

Step 1: Relaxation Association.
(KEY)
Step 2: Basic Self Analysis Question.
"What was my level of relaxation on
my good shots and on my bad shots

and how did I get relaxed or was relaxation even a problem?''

Step 3: Rehearse a Positive *Imag Actor.*
e.g. See an image rehearsal sequence or your relaxation procedure out on the golf course. Refresh your subconscious by letting it 'see' you as a relaxed golfer.

Example 5

Step 1: Thought Stopping and Negative
(KEY) Statements.
Step 2: Basic Self Analysis Question.
''How does my game analysis look for those occasions when I had to stop and replace negative thoughts with pictorially positive images for those occasions?''
Step 3: Rehearse a Positive *Imag Actor.*
See your thought stopping procedure in a set of mental images when you firmly carry out your procedure.

Other keys that you could use for post game analysis are:

1. high and low emotional states;
2. maintenance of positive images;
3. mental rehearsal situations (did you rehearse or not?);
4. mental rehearsal of your best golf qualities;
5. common irrational beliefs;
6. situational over competitiveness.

Suggested Further Readings: Chapter 11, Psychological Foundations of Sport, Silva and Weinberg, Editors, Human Kinetics Publishers, 1984, Champaign, Illinois, USA.

Check your golf after your game when you are relaxed

Post Game Analysis for Checking Your Specific Imagery

The following entries from a post game diary analysis stress a few common problems that tend to develop with the application of *Imagexercise©* in game situations.

The use of a diary to record such problems works well if the golfer analyzes soon after a golf game.

Of course, it is helpful to discuss the problems with other golfers in your group. Focus on the correctness of the decisions you made on the golf course. In all cases you have carried out the left brain analyzer procedure and have properly attempted to use the right brain or Performance selector to carry out your shot. Your ability to use vivid images that can be held in your mind's eye is assured after working on Chapter 4.

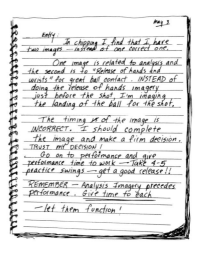

Common Problems of Golf Imagery

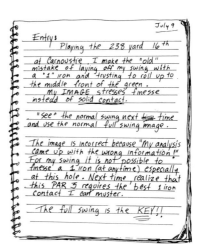

What Golfers Say About Imagery For Golf

Imagexercise© and *exercising* can help concentration because it helps to take your mind off previous bad shots or shots of other players or other things going through your mind. Proper *Imagexercise*© can also eliminate negative thinking. By thinking only of how excellent a shot you are going to make and by imagining yourself striking center to center shots and seeing the ball go directly to target, you eliminate all negative images. This relaxes you and keeps you from getting uptight and frustrated. If you hit better on the driving range than on the golf course then use imagery to take you to the range and play as if you were there and not having any pressure at all.

▪ *Imagexercise©* *improved* my game in a number of ways. It really changed my pre game mental set on the way to the golf course. I learned to concentrate on the right things at the appropriate time.

▪ *Imagexercise©* put focus into my golf game and I concentrated on what improved my golf, not on opponents and what those watching me might be doing.

▪ Taking one's time in golf through such things as no rush-rush imagery lets you block out personal problems and relax oneself by deep breathing and control to get rid of muscle tension. Imagery-golf allowed me to have a positive attitude in golf and let me give myself positive feedback.

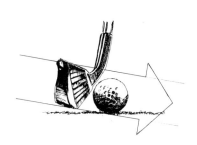

▪ For me and my golf, imagery meant using the image of Tom Watson's golf swing and learning how to copy it consistently. Also, I now stand behind the ball before hitting it and use an imagery routine. It helps.

▪ I found I used proper posture in golf better. The rhythm of my swing was totally in control with imagery.

▪ First of all, you must not be in a hurry and I learned to use imagery to 'trick' my subconscious into thinking that I am organized and patient. Use imagery to slow down. For *Imagexercise©* to work out on the course, I learned that I must have seen and practiced certain shots. My log book proved to be extremely beneficial.

▪ After reading *IMAGES FOR GOLF,* I started having some knowledge with me from the last game I played. I started to understand the concept of Imagery golf. Being able to recall and apply what I had already seen and learned aided me tremendously in preparing the next shot. Although I am not very accurate with imagery yet, I used it frequently to guide my concentration.

▪ The benefit of *Imagexercise©* golf for me lay largely in pre scouting and finding optimal landing areas for each shot. I feel a golfer can improve each time out, even on a course that one plays often. It seems there is always one shot or one hole that escapes our ability every time. It is this challenge that can be boldly confronted by this method of planning for best ball placement. This is a definite aid to the golfer and a good exercise.

▪ I soon learned that from the teebox there are many obstacles and hazards you can not see in golf. Through imagery and scouting I soon started being knowledgeable about the course I played. To play low on the pin helped my putting. I used imagery to relax my swing and to gain better balance (an outstanding skier talking). I seemed to learn how to get feel in my golf swing.

▪ It is annoying when you hit beautiful shots at the driving range and terrible ones on the golf course. I have to not be so psyched up on the golf course. You create pressure on yourself because at the range you don't aim as carefully. Imagery started to allow me to use an aiming system and get rid of my former frustrations in golf.

▪ On the 5th hole, a slight dogleg Par 4, to a green that sits up like an elevated island, with traps just below the green, big trees and a narrow fairway, I really used successful imagery. Here is how I remember it happening: I visualize the approach shot as high and landing and stopping at center green. My positive image disregards the slopes all around the green. There it is that wonderful 7 iron. The shot lands 10 feet from the pin just as I saw it! The putt just about gives birdie. (Maybe I'll be a golfer yet!)

CHAPTER FOUR
SUMMARY OF THE CHAPTER

▪ The techniques for producing and controlling images are explained and illustrated in Chapter 4.

- Effective sports performances are clearly linked up with imagery ability.

- The discovery or improvement of visualization/imagery is possible for most people.

- With time the golfer athlete can expect to become proficient in the use of image skill.

- Golfers have reported lower golf scores by simply reading about visualizing in golf, but to organize and practice imagery golf as laid out in Chapter 4 can provide sure score reduction.

- Simple guidelines are reviewed for pure visualizing ability.

- Seventeen progressive image building exercises are available complete with golf practice examples.

- Tips for image exercising and relaxing your body are explained.

- How to set up reasonable goals for practicing is outlined.

- Training time, completing an imagery bank, over-concentration and common pitfalls are developed.

- Two types of post game analysis are included.

- The Chapter is finished with discussions and reactions of golfers to *Imagexercise©*.

Appendix

Appendix 1
Other Imagery Books and Articles For Resource Reading

Arieti, S. *Creativity: The Magic Synthesis.* New York: Basic Books, 1976.

Berger, P., Berger, B., and Kellner, H. *The Homeless Mind.* New York: Vintage, 1974.

Gordon, R.A. A Very Private World. In: P.W. Sheehan (Ed.) *The Function and Nature of Mental Imagery.* New York: Academic Press, 1972.

Heilbrun, C. *Re-Inventing Womanhood.* New York: Norton, 1979.

Jacobsen, E. Electrical Measurements of Neuro-muscular States During Mental Activities. *American Journal of Physiology,* 95 (1930).

Carney, R. How Denis Watson Broke Through. *Golf Digest,* (December, 1984).

Peper, G. Voodoo Doctors (What's Inside). *Golf Magazine,* 12 (1984).

Hogan, C. Exercising the Image Muscle. *Golf Magazine,* 2 (1985).

Hogan, C., Van Delsam, D. and Davis, S., *5 Days to Golf Excellence.* Lake Oswego, Oregon. Merl Miller Associates, 1986.

Appendix 2
Index of Imagexercise© and New Golf Terms For Imagery Golfers

creative subconscious
word pictures
sport arousal
sport science expert
sport psychology
coming attraction IE
visualization
optic golf ball
muscle memory
IE system
golf eyesight

external IE
internal IE
pure golfer

focused awareness
databank of IEs
vividness and IE
intimidation in golf
golf realism
Technique IE
Tactics IE
Tenacity IE

intuition golf
ball speed IEing
tracking sub skills
hit through visualizing
no rush-rush IE
patience IE
waggle IE
IE warm-up
golf vision warm-up
Introductory golfer, Occasional golfer
Regular golfer, Low handicap amateur golfer

replay imagery
small accomplishment health
small accomplishment fitness
small accomplishment flexibility
National Golf Foundation (NGF)
Gallweys' back hit
long-range IE program
child prodigy golfer
subconscious golf

Appendix 3
Suggested Weight Training and Conditioning Golf Program

I. Flexibility Without Weights

1. Elbow Pull Overhead and Side Stretch
   (alternate slow stretch each way)

2. Elbow Pull Behind Head
   (alternate slow stretch)

3. Pull "Front Golf Arm" Up Under Chin
   (slow stretch; with shoulder turn as exercise takes a golf-like position; alternate as if you are a right-handed and then a left-handed golfer)

4. Slow Golf Swing with Resistance
(use other arm to provide resistance and stress arm action, body action, and hand/wrist action) Do this near the hitting area of the golf swing.

II. Flexibility with Weights or Machines such as Nautilus

Use the three basic Nautilus exercises for shoulders or substitute partner resistance for the same exercises (as below).

5. Shoulder Adduction/Abduction
(Elbows to side, shoulder high hands/arms up) Bring elbows together, move elbows apart (maximum stretch), use light weights and many repetitions. (On the *Nautilus* machine Exercise #5 is commonly called a *Pectoral* or *Pecs* exercise.)

6. Pullovers (forward and backward)
Hands back as far as they can stretch; weight at shoulders, elbows straight ahead, pull to stomach. Repeat (light weights, maximum repetitions) (*Nautilus/* pullover machine)

7. Double Arm Lift
(Fists together; lift arms from stomach up to forehead area) On the *Nautilus* this is called the "Butterfly."

III. Legs and Lower Body

8. Choose between the following: ride stationary bike; jog; ride regular bike; use leg resistance machines (e.g., Hydra Gym is good). Do a lot of sit-ups. Use a climbing wall (low horizontal moves) if available.

IV. Swing a Weighted Golf Club

9. Consider this as a basic exercise for a golfer. Swing the club daily, stressing the stretch to visualized maximum. Do this when travelling.

Bibliography and Resources

Chapter 1

1. Bennett, J. and Pravitz, J. *The Miracle of Sports Psychology*. Englewood Cliffs: Prentice Hall, 1982.

2. Ferguson, M. *The Aquarian Conspiracy*. Los Angeles: J.P. Tarcher, 1980. (distributed by Houghton Mifflin, Boston)

3. Coop, R. and Wiren, G. *The New Golf Mind*. Norwalk, Conn.: Golf Digest Special Services, 1978.

4. Suinn, R. Body thinking: psychology for Olympic champs. *Psychology Today* (July, 1976).

5. Schmidt, R. *Motor Control and Learning*. Champaign, Ill.: Human Kinetics Publishers, 1982.

6. Lucas, G. Imagery strategies and their impact on shotmaking accuracy and game score in golf. Paper read at the Los Angeles Pre-Olympic Scientific Congress, 1984.

7. Harris, D. and Harris, B. *Sport Psychology: Mental Skills for Physical People*. New York: Leisure Press, 1984.

8. Jacobsen, E. *Progressive Relaxation*. Chicago: University of Chicago Press, 1938.

9. Brown, B. *Supermind: The Ultimate Energy*. New York: Harper and Row, 1980.
10. Canada's Moe Norman. *Golf Digest* (1978).
11. Sperry. In: Galyean, B.C. Guided imagery in the curriculum. *Education Leadership* (March 1983).
12. Bogen. In: Galyean, B.C. Guided imagery in the curriculum. *Education Leadership* (March 1983).

Chapter 2

1. Miller, J. and Shankland, D. *Pure Golf*. Garden City, N.Y.: Doubleday, 1976.
2. Gallwey, T. *Inner Tennis*. New York: Random House, 1977.
3. Maltz, M. *Psycho-Cybernetics*. Englewood Cliffs: Prentice Hall, 1960.
4. Grant, E. *Subconscious Golf*. Tempe, Arizona: Mindgame Enterprises, 1977.
5. Rotella, R.J. and Bunker, L. *Mind Mastery for Winning Golf*. Englewood Cliffs: Prentice Hall, 1981.
6. Hogan, B. and Ravielli, A. *The Modern Fundamentals of Golf*. Cranbury, N.J.: A.S. Barnes, 1957.
7. Murphy, M. *The Psychic Side of Sport*. Reading, Me.: Addison-Wesley, 1978.

Chapter 3

1. Cobb, N., Kahn, A., Kath, S. *How Your Self Image Controls Your Tennis Game*. Psychology Today, June 1977.
2. Morgan, W.P. *Prediction of Performance in Athletics*. In Klovora, P., Daniel, J.V. (Eds) Coach, Athlete, and the Sport Psychologist. Toronto: University of Toronto Press, 1979.
3. Fisher, A.C. *New Directions in Sport Personality Research*. In Silva, J., Weinberg, R.S. (Eds) Psychological Foundations of Sport. Champaign, Illinois: Human Kinetics Publishers, 1984.

Other Resources:

3. Evans, W. *Encyclopedia of Golf*. London: Robert Hale and Company, 1971.

Chapter 4

1. Singer, Jerome. *Daydreaming.* New York: Random House, 1966.

2. McKim, R., *Experience in Visual Thinking.* Belmont, California: Wadsworth Publishing, 1972.

3. Horowitz, M. *Image Formation and Cognition.* New York: Appleton Century-Crofts, 1970.

4. Castenada, C. *Tales of Power.* New York: Simon and Schuster, 1974.

5. Weihl, Andrew. *Creative Visualization.* New York: Greenwich Book Publishing, 1958.

6. Brown, Barbara. *New Mind, New Body.* New York: Harper Row Co, 1974. (see also Brown, Barbara. *Supermind: The Ultimate Energy.* already listed).